Diana Wright is the Personal Fir
of *The Sunday Times*. Her prev
include, *A Guide to Mortgages*,
Lump Sum Investment and *A H   Great
Britain*. In 1995 she was awarded a Golden Pen Award
for Personal Finance Journalism sponsored by the Co-
operative Bank, being voted the Journalists' Journalist
of the Year.

Diana Wright is the series editor for *The Sunday Times
Personal Finance Guides*.

Also available in this series:

The Sunday Times Personal Finance Guide to Your Pension
BY STEPHEN ELLIS

The Sunday Times Personal Finance Guide to The Protection Game
BY KEVIN PRATT

The Sunday Times Personal Finance Guide to Your Retirement
BY DIANA WRIGHT

The Sunday Times Personal Finance Guide to Tax-free Savings
BY CHRISTOPHER GILCHRIST

THE SUNDAY TIMES
Personal Finance Guide to

YOUR HOME

How to Buy, Sell and Pay for It

Diana Wright

HarperCollins*Publishers*

HarperCollins*Publishers*,
77–85 Fulham Palace Road,
Hammersmith, London W6 8JB

A Paperback Original 1996
3 5 7 9 8 6 4

Copyright © Editor – Diana Wright 1996
© Author – Diana Wright 1996
© Book – Times Newspapers Ltd 1996

The Author asserts the moral right to
be identified as the author of this work

No responsibility for loss occasioned to any person acting
or refraining from action as a result of any material in this publication
can be accepted by the editor, author, publisher or *The Sunday Times*

A catalogue record for this book
is available from the British Library

ISBN 0 00 638704 7

Set in Linotron Times by
Rowland Phototypesetting Limited,
Bury St Edmunds, Suffolk

Printed and bound in Great Britain by
Caledonian International Book Manufacturing Ltd, Glasgow

CONTENTS

ACKNOWLEDGEMENTS

I am grateful to the many organizations and companies who have provided information and figures for this book; sources have been quoted where applicable. I would particularly like to thank the press officers of the Halifax, Nationwide and Woolwich building societies for handling an endless stream of queries with patience and efficiency. Thanks are also due to mortgage brokers John Charcol Limited and London & Country Mortgages and, finally, to Doreen Fitzgerald, for first-class secretarial support.

INTRODUCTION

Anyone who still thinks that a house is 'the best investment you'll ever make' must have been living on a desert island for the last few years. Most of us know better; for some of us, the price of that knowledge has been very high indeed. A rising tide of repossessions and spiralling mortgage debts has contributed more horror-stories than most people ever want or need to read.

But for all that, most people in this country own their own homes, or aspire to. We find the alternatives – spending one's life in private rented accommodation, or dependent on the whims and waiting lists of local councils – an even worse prospect to face than the perils of property ownership. And despite all the problems, there's something *nice* about owning your own place: you can choose – within reason – where you live; you can decorate it to your own taste; and after half a lifetime, maybe, of paying a mortgage, the place is utterly and indubitably yours – you can live there 'rent free' for the rest of your life.

Whoever first coined the phrase, 'An Englishman's home is his castle' would get thoroughly hauled over the PC coals today. But there it is, we Great Britons like owning our own home, and we have been influenced by a whole range of factors, both historic and economic: post-war inflation; the rise, during the last century, of the mutual self-help associations known as building societies, which helped thousands of working-class Victorians to escape the clutches of greedy landlords; and then the anti-landlord legislation of the last 30 years, which has slashed the supply of decent property to rent.

This love affair with property is a great deal cooler in other parts of the world. According to the Council of Mortgage Lenders, at the top of the European league of homeownership, perhaps surprisingly, are Ireland and Greece, where 80%-plus are homeowners, but Great Britain is not that far behind at around 68%. Switzerland, that bastion of financial self-righteousness and fiscal stability, has one of the lowest scores; at the last count (some five years ago) just 30% of the population were homeowners. In Germany the score was around 40%, and the Netherlands were not much higher, at 46%.

Most of us will be quite content to leave the Swiss burghers in their snug rented homes: we want to buy. And, surprisingly perhaps, the situation for buyers is better now than it has been for many years. If you had been a clairvoyant in the late 1980s or even the early 1990s, you might, like the old local asked by a traveller how to get to a nearby village, have told a prospective homebuyer, 'Well if I were you, I wouldn't start from here.'

But these days, you *can* 'start from here'. You can forget – if it ever crossed your mind – about property being the instant route to riches. You can forget the old advice about borrowing as much as you can possibly afford. You can even forget about the vital importance of getting 'on the first rung of the property ladder' – as if once you'd made that first step, you could gallop up the rest just like a clockwork toy.

Instead, if you want reassurance that 'starting from here' is not a bad idea, have a look at Figure 1 produced by the Halifax Building Society. In retrospect, the rise in house prices during the last half of the 1980s looks like a crazy aberration. Ultimately, house prices must be governed by what people are willing to pay, and what they are willing to pay is in itself governed by what they *can* pay. With house prices rising so much faster than earnings, it now seems clear – with hindsight – that the crunch was inevitable. True, things looked different at the time – but we're older and wiser now.

But anyone buying today must have niggling worries: house prices are lower now, and we've learned that particular lesson; it's obviously not a bad time to buy; but are there other major pitfalls with buying a property which will only emerge later on?

Figure 1: House price trends

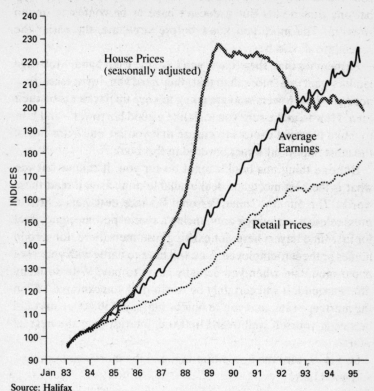

Source: Halifax

The answer is that there are always pitfalls (it couldn't really be otherwise) when you embark on such a major financial transaction: a property will cost maybe three times your total annual income, and if you make a mistake you will not only have to live *with* it, but live *in* it for a good few years.

The main purpose of this book is to highlight those pitfalls, on the principle that forewarned is forearmed. If you are new to homebuying you may well find that entire process lengthy and confusing: we are led to believe that it is the third most stress-inducing experience after divorce and a death in the family. Unless you are extremely lucky – buying a newly built house with a convenient cash pile for example – the process is almost certain to be long drawn-out. But it doesn't have to be confusing or too stressful. The more you know before you start, the easier the procedure should be.

Remember that, these days, *you* have the whip hand. Mortgage lenders want you; more than that, they *need* you – or at least, they need good borrowers who are going to keep up payments on their loan. How to make sure you look like a good borrower – and how to make the right choices to ensure that you *are* one – are two of the most important topics covered in this book.

But one thing this book cannot do for you: it cannot tell you what is the best mortgage deal available now, as you read these words. *The Sunday Times* Personal Finance desk gets a pile of press releases each week announcing a special new mortgage deal for first-time buyers here, for existing customers there, for second homes or the self-employed. You will have to battle with your own paper-mountain when you actually come to buy. With so many offers around, it will certainly be worth it: if you can save 1% on the mortgage rate, and you're borrowing, say, £50,000, you could be saving yourself well over £10,000 in interest over the next 25 years.

So get on with the house-hunting, and the mortgage-hunting – and good luck!

1 | *First Catch Your Home*

It may seem like stating the obvious, but the very first thing you need to do before you even start wading through the pile of estate agents' blurb is to work out what your price range is. Unless you have an unusual degree of self-control, you are unlikely to stick at the bottom end of what you can afford; so often it seems that, with just a few thousand pounds more, you could buy somewhere so much nicer.

These days it is not a good idea to borrow right up to the hilt, on the premise that high inflation will soon whittle away the loan's real value. But there is still a good case for spending that little bit extra if it means you can buy a place you will really be happy in. Buying a house not only costs money (for a detailed estimate, turn to Chapter 3, page 32); it costs time and effort and, as anyone who has been through it will tell you, the sheer pain of packing up all your worldly goods and shifting them from one place to another is not something you want to repeat every couple of years.

If this is your first buy, start out looking for a place you reckon you could live in for at least the next five or, better, the next ten years. If you are tempted by a place you think you'll grow out of (for whatever reason – financially, socially) within the next couple of years, then you should ask yourself why you are proposing to buy it instead of renting.

How Much Can You Afford?

For maybe 99% of first-time buyers, and plenty of second-timers, too, this question boils down to 'How much will someone lend me?' There are two basic rules that lenders follow when they decide how much to lend in any given case. The first relates to the borrower's income; the second, to the percentage of the purchase price or valuation of the property.

Borrower's income

For many years now, most mortgage lenders have followed a simple rule on the maximum loan they will give, which runs:

either (a): three times the first income and once times the second income;

or (b): two and a half times the joint incomes.

That gives you a fairly simple sum to do: if you are buying on your own and your salary is £20,000, you can borrow £60,000. As a couple, if one partner is earning £25,000, the other £15,000, you could borrow £90,000 under the first rule, or £100,000 under the second. The closer your earnings are, the more rule (b) will allow you to borrow. For instance: if you are both earning £30,000, you could borrow £150,000 under rule (b) but only £120,000 under rule (a). But if one partner is earning £60,000 and the other just £10,000, the joint incomes rule yields a total loan of £175,000 while rule (a) makes for a maximum loan of £190,000.

If you are determined to borrow more, you should be able to find some ways round this maximum. For instance, at the time of writing, many of the big building societies were routinely offering up to three and a quarter times the first income. The absolute maximum I have been able to find is four times a single income, or three and a quarter times joint incomes.

These sort of multiples are not to be had merely for the asking. The 'mainstream' lenders – the high street banks and building societies – will probably not consider lending at such levels; some of the smaller, specialist lenders may do so. You may well need the help of a good **mortgage broker**, and you will still be unlikely to succeed unless, firstly, you have a large cash deposit to put down, and secondly, you are in a secure job with prospects of promotion and big pay rises in the near future.

It is surprising, in many ways, that lenders have stuck for so long to the 'multiples of income' criteria for assessing how much to lend. We all know people who somehow manage to save large sums of money out of an apparently small income – and others who have no trouble running through whatever they're paid and more. It does not take a genius to work out that a married man with a non-earning wife, a big loan on the car and two children at private school will have much less income available to pay mortgage interest than a single woman with no children or car.

Indeed, a few lenders have abandoned the 'multiples' basis entirely in favour of a detailed assessment of what a particular individual can afford. They take the after-tax income, deducting all regular outgoings including, for example, personal loan payments, maintenance payments, school fees and council tax, to arrive at a net figure on which they base their lending decision. This approach makes much more sense, and it will be surprising if the majority of lenders don't change their policy along these lines in the near future.

Property price or valuation

However large their income, borrowers are expected to have some cash of their own to put down on the property, and the greater the percentage borrowed, the more expensive it usually is. The figure lenders work from is not necessarily the price that a buyer has agreed to pay, but the lender's valuation of the property, which is often lower (I have never heard of a case where it has been higher).

Borrowing up to 75% of a property's value is usually no problem. Of course, many people need to borrow more. In 1994 the average for first-time buyers was around 89%, according to the Halifax Building Society, and for those buying a second or subsequent time, slightly less than 75%.

Once the loan rises above 75% extra costs come into play, notably the mortgage indemnity guarantee, a one-off payment which gets progressively bigger the higher the percentage of valuation that the loan represents (see Chapter 7, page 81). Since the end of the property boom most mainstream lenders have restricted their absolute maximum to 95%. It is possible to get 100% loans (see page 82), but not easy.

How Much Should You Afford?

You may find a lender who is willing to make you a mortgage offer, but is it a good idea to accept it? At *The Sunday Times* we still get letters from readers who believe that their problems with spiralling credit card debts or mortgage arrears are caused by the bank or the building society which loaned them the money in the first place. These readers do have a point: I believe the availability of easy credit – not just on offer, but aggressively marketed, in a constant stream of junk mail – has caused an awful lot of heartache over the last few years, and the lenders must take some of the blame for that.

But do remember that, as far as mortgage lenders are concerned, the only thing they've got to sell is *money*. After all, that's their business, and in many ways it's just like any other. John Lewis, for example, will allow you to purchase anything in their store, but you don't have to buy up the entire contents every time you go in. So also with mortgages: *you* must decide how much you want to borrow, and rely on your own judgement, not the lender's, about what you'll feel happy with.

If you are buying as a couple it is particularly important to look ahead a few years. Lenders are strictly non-sexist these days, and the 'first' income is deemed to be the biggest, whether it is earned by the woman or the man. But if you are planning to have children in a few years, at which point one of you will probably give up work or go part-time, it would be unwise to borrow significantly on the strength of that income. This is only common sense, of course, but do bear these factors in mind.

As mentioned before, this 'three times income' rule is rather a curious one. Not so long ago, in 1990, mortgage rates stood at

15.4%. Today they are much lower: at the time of writing the basic variable rate charged by most lenders stood at 8.35%. In 1990, if you borrowed on a variable rate of interest, then your monthly interest payments on a £50,000 loan were approximately £545, including the full basic rate tax relief available at the time. Today the interest payments amount to just £317 a month.

Unfortunately, a rise in interest rates doesn't mean that your income also stretches. While you might have no problem meeting a monthly mortgage bill of £317, a jump to £545 could be very hard to live with. So whatever the theoretical maximum you can borrow, look at the monthly payments – and be prepared for a rise in rates.

Borrowing costs
Table 1 gives you an initial indication of monthly payments on a standard 25-year mortgage (see page 10) at a whole range of interest rates (Chapter 3, page 32, will go into more detail about the various mortgage options open to borrowers). The table is split into two parts because you are still allowed tax relief on mortgage interest payments for the first £30,000 of capital borrowed to purchase your main home. It shows the monthly costs for a standard 25 year repayment mortgage (see page 44), and also the interest-only costs for borrowers who are taking out a Pep or endowment mortgage (see pages 61 and 55). Don't forget that the monthly cost of the Pep or endowment premiums must be added to the interest figure to arrive at an overall cost.

Currently, the rate of tax relief available is 15%, and this is automatically knocked off your interest payments – even if you don't pay income tax. This system is known as MIRAS (Mortgage Interest Relief At Source). On the rest of the loan you must pay the full gross interest. The monthly payment shown here is for every £1,000 borrowed.

You can, of course, escape at least some of the uncertainty by opting for a fixed-rate mortgage rather than a variable-rate one (see page 33).

Table 1: The monthly costs of mortgage payments per £1,000 borrowed

Interest Rate	Repayment		Interest Only	
	NET	GROSS	NET	GROSS
%	£	£	£	£
6	5.77	6.52	4.25	5.00
7	6.28	7.15	4.96	5.83
8	6.81	7.81	5.67	6.67
9	7.36	8.48	6.38	7.50
10	7.93	9.18	7.08	8.33
11	8.52	9.90	7.79	9.17
12	9.12	10.62	8.50	10.00
13	9.74	11.37	9.21	10.83
14	10.37	12.12	9.92	11.67
15	11.02	12.89	10.63	12.50
8.35*	7.00	8.04	5.91	6.96

* *The most common basic variable rate charged at the time of writing.*
Source: Halifax

Extra costs of homeowning

If you are new to homebuying, remember that the monthly mortgage is only one bill among many that will be dropping through your new letter box. There will be the local authority council tax, water rates, and telephone, gas and electricity bills to pay. Then there is buildings and contents insurance (see pages 118 and 120) and, if you have bought a flat rather than a house, probably a regular service charge as well.

Hunting Your House

Once you know what your price range is you can start house-hunting in earnest. Clearly, it is impossible to tell other people what property they should buy: it is a matter of personal taste and individual circumstances. Nevertheless, it is worth listening to what the professionals – the estate agents and surveyors – have to say on the subject. One point which they are all agreed on is expressed in the old estate agent's dictum: 'There are three things that count with houses. In order of importance, they are: position, position and position.'

The point seems so obvious as scarcely to be worth mentioning. But in fact 'position' is not just a matter of whether your property is in a 'good' area or a nice tree-lined street; it covers all sorts of other factors which may be of crucial importance to you: is it in the catchment area for a good school? How far away are the shops – will you have to make an expedition every time you run out of milk? What is it like for public transport; how long will your commuting times be? Is the local train service adequate, indifferent or downright bad?

If those are the macro-factors of position, there are micro-factors as well: which way does the house itself face? Will it get the sun, or will you be living in permanent semi-darkness? Is there a factory down the road – out of sight, maybe – whose smells are going to be a permanent, and unwelcome, part of your future life? Is it in the flight path of a major airport? Some of these drawbacks are going to hit you between the eyes as soon as you see a place, but others may take more digging to unearth. The moral is to keep your eyes, ears – and nose! – open as you go round.

One useful suggestion, particularly if you are buying in a town rather than the suburbs or country, is to visit the place both during the daytime and in the evening to check on the availability of parking. If you are close to some outlet for evening entertainment and the house does not provide off-street parking, you could be in for daily irritation as you struggle to find a parking spot when you get home from work. And while you're looking at the cars on the street, check their makes and registration numbers; you can take it too far, but car-spotting is a good basis for a few educated guesses about the sort of people who live in that area.

Finally, it might be an idea to take a compass with you, so you can check whether the 'south-facing garden' really is what it says. You might, of course, be house-hunting on a sunny day – but we can hardly rely on that in the UK.

Some estate agents suggest that buyers should put down in writing a list of their requirements, including the number of bedrooms, living rooms and so on. This might seem excessive, but it can be a useful exercise if you go on to prioritize those requirements. The Perfect House probably doesn't exist (at least not in your price range – whatever that may be) and buyers may well need to think hard about the factors they are prepared to compromise on, and those they are not.

Internal decorations and fitments have not even been mentioned yet, and with good reason. It is always possible – albeit at some expense – to rip out some perfectly foul kitchen or bathroom; what you cannot do is pick up the house and move it three miles down the road. And although it is tempting – particularly if you are moving from another property – to see, first and foremost, whether your cherished three-piece suite will fit into the living room, you need to remember that a piece of furniture is a good deal less expensive than a house, and this should really come fairly low down the list of priorities.

Old or new property?

Some people wouldn't dream of buying problem-filled old houses; others turn their noses up at anything later than Edwardian. Really old houses – by which I mean a century or more – can indeed have all sorts of problems: high ceilings mean high heating bills; slate roofs can mean the constant (and expensive) attentions of a roofer; the basic layout of the rooms often reflects the upstairs-downstairs life lived in those days, resulting in dark, poky kitchens which are hardly going to be appreciated by those who have to do the washing up and cooking today.

But if you are a devotee of old houses nothing anyone can say will put you off, and indeed, being a member of that camp myself, I wouldn't want to. Bear in mind, however, that the house may be listed for conservation purposes: any subsequent alterations could be extremely expensive or even impossible.

From a resale point of view, the 'problem' houses are not those built 60 or 100 years ago, but the 20- or 30-year-old properties. It may be unfair to generalize, but nowadays we perceive houses built during the 1960s and 1970s as very unsympathetic – 'all soulless open-plan jobs', as one estate agent described them, without so much as an open fire to make them homely or welcoming.

House-building in the 1990s seems to have come back into line with what people actually want, but a word of caution is in order here as well. If you are buying within a development where second and third phases are due to be built later, and you expect to sell within a few years, do remember that your home may have to compete with similar, but brand-new, properties down the road.

First-time buyers should also think hard about whether it is wise to buy what used to be called 'starter homes': studio flats or tiny one-bedroom houses. These made sense in times of high house-price inflation because they allowed borrowers to build up equity in their property almost automatically. But today there seems little point in buying such a home unless you are anticipating living in it long term. Most starter homes are designed for people who will be staying there a few years and then moving on, in which case, bearing in mind the costs of purchase and sale, there seems little point in buying rather than renting. This has convinced many housing market analysts that such homes do not in general represent a good buy, unless they are so cheap that mortgage costs are a great deal lower than the equivalent rent.

Finally, potential buyers must take account of the physical structure of the property. If they are really serious about a property they should commission a proper independent survey before making a final offer, and that should bring any problems to light. There are some obvious points to watch out for, which can be spotted even on a first visit. These might be enough to put you off and save money and time in the long run.

Tips from surveyors include the following:

- Take a pair of binoculars with you to look at the state of the roof and chimneys. Check whether there are any slates or tiles obviously missing; is there a good 'ridge line' on the roof? Be wary of flat roofs, which can require frequent and expensive maintenance. Likewise, roofs which have 'valleys' rather than ridges – often found on pre-1870s properties – can also cause problems as water collects in the valley and will find any weak spot to seep through.

  Is the roof made of slate? If so, and the property is old rather than brand new, you may be in for some large bills sooner or later. The slate itself can last almost indefinitely, but the nails that fix it to the house can deteriorate and at some point a completely new roof may be needed.

- Check out the main walls of the house for bulges and cracks. If cracks look old, there may be no need to worry. Many houses have old settlement or subsidence cracks which developed during their first few years of settling, or even – in London, and a few other cities – after bomb damage during the last war. But new-looking cracks could be a cause for concern; the problem may get worse and require costly underpinning.

- Look for the signs of damp and ask whether the house has a damp-proof course. Check on the state of the drainpipes and guttering; look to see if there are any damp patches either outside or inside, on the walls or ceilings.

  One surveyor has even suggested that buyers should take a small pen-knife with them and prod wooden skirting boards or window frames to check for damp. If the knife goes in easily, without resistance, that means problems. But if you do so, I would suggest you do it as unobtrusively as possible, otherwise you will encounter problems of a more immediate nature as irate owners accuse you of malicious damage to their home!

How to get the best out of estate agents
Having established a price range, serious house-hunters will then
head for the local estate agents. It is only logical to sign up, so to
speak, with all the agents active in the area and get onto their
mailing lists.

Estate agents are agents for the seller, not the buyer, but recent
legislation has imposed on them some legal duties towards the
purchaser as well. The Property Misdescriptions Act 1991 was a
well-intentioned piece of legislation aimed at stopping the worst of
estate agent hyperbole – the 'picturesque cottage with superb
aspects' which turns out to be a grubby and broken-down end-of-
terrace facing an equally grubby playground. The net result,
however, is that agents' details are probably less informative than
they used to be. In the early days of the act one big firm of estate
agents claimed it would no longer include train journey times to
London in the information it sent out to prospective customers
because these so often turned out to be totally inaccurate!

But in any case, there are no real short-cuts in the house-hunting
business, and agents' lists can only give an indication of whether a
property might be suitable for you.

Buyers do have some rights: agents must treat all prospective
buyers equally, and must not 'invent' other interested parties in
order to spur you on to make an offer; they cannot give as fact
details that they do not themselves know for sure, such as the
length remaining on a lease. However, they do not have to
volunteer information that might be detrimental to their client's
(the seller's) cause.

This means the onus is on you to ask the questions. With older
houses in particular, they should include the following:

- Has the house been underpinned, and if so, when?
- Is there a damp-proof course?
- Have the window frames been renewed recently?
- When was the house last rewired, and was that full or
  partial?

● Has the roof been renewed, and if so, when?

You are also quite entitled to ask – either of the agent or, more likely, the seller – for details of recent heating and lighting bills, council tax and water rates.

Professional bodies

Many firms of agents are members of a professional organization which can help to sort out problems if matters go seriously awry. Around half the UK's 12,000-odd estate agency branches belong to the National Association of Estate Agents; in addition there is the Royal Institute of Chartered Surveyors, and the Incorporated Society of Valuers and Auctioneers (see Appendix, page 132). All have codes of conduct and formal complaints mechanisms.

Most of the big chains of estate agents – those owned by banks, building societies or life assurance companies – are members of OCEA, the Ombudsman for Corporate Estate Agents (see Appendix, page 135), which is an independent body whose purpose is to handle complaints.

Buying by auction

If you are prepared for a bit of a gamble, buying by auction might save you 20% or more of the normal market price of a property. The drawback is that you may pay out money for surveys and initial legal fees with no guarantee that the property will be yours at the end of the day – or, worse, you may get carried away during the sale and end up bidding far too much! If you are considering this route, have a few dry runs and attend some auctions as an observer first.

Successful bidders are contractually obliged to buy the property; they must usually put up 10% of the price on the auction day itself – in cash or a banker's draft – and produce the balance within 28 days. This means you must organize mortgage finance, carry out a survey and get the necessary legal checks done before the bidding starts. Telephone bids are sometimes accepted, and it is usually possible to make an offer before the day of the auction, although you may not get quite such a bargain.

The Incorporated Society of Valuers and Auctioneers (see Appendix, page 132) can provide details of property auctioneers.

Relocating

An estimated 90%-plus of house purchases are made within a five- or 10-mile radius of where the purchaser already lives, but there are always individuals or families who have to uproot and move to distant parts of the country, usually following job relocations.

House-hunting hundreds of miles away is very much more difficult; the questions that need to be asked about a new area are very much harder to answer at a distance.

This is where a good estate agent should be able to help. According to the chairman of the National Association of Estate Agents, competent estate agents should be able to provide information sheets on their local area, including the whereabouts of shops, transport facilities and the catchment areas for good schools. Around 500 firms under the NAEA umbrella belong to an organization called Homelink which refers house-hunters to the appropriate local agents. For more information contact the NAEA itself (see Appendix, page 132).

A second body, the Association of Relocation Agents (see Appendix page 132), represents companies whose sole business is helping people to relocate. Unlike estate agents, relocation companies represent the buyer, not the seller. They will do the initial house-hunting for you and, being armed with local knowledge, should be able to save you not just a great deal of time, but money too. Members of the association use a variety of charging methods, from flat fees to a percentage of the property value. As an indication, the bill from a relocation agent is likely to be at least £1,250 or around 1 to 1.5% of the purchase price. The association will provide a list of members free of charge.

Hunting the Mortgage

Mortgage lenders need you – and there are at least 140 of them looking for business. It is certainly worth taking the time to track down the best of the current mortgage offers, or using a good firm of mortgage brokers. Brokers may be especially useful if your requirements are out of the ordinary – for example, if you need a 100% loan. Some of the larger brokers can sometimes also negotiate special packages which are not available to the general public. (For a more detailed discussion of mortgages and lenders, see Chapter 3, page 32.)

Obviously this book cannot provide details of the various mortgage deals on offer at the time you want to buy; lenders change their offers all the time – with fixed rate loans a particular rate may be on offer for only a matter of weeks, until the sum allocated to it has been used up.

A stroll down your local high street could provide details of dozens of different mortgage offers – fixed or discounted rates, cash rebate offers or money off legal expenses. However, these days the so-called 'high-street' lenders – the banks and building societies – only represent a part of the business. Telephone-based mortgage lenders are beginning to appear. Some, like Direct Line and First Direct, are part of an organization whose business is conducted exclusively over the phone; others, like Bradford & Bingley Direct, are an offshoot of a traditional lender. This type of business, with lower overheads and no properties to maintain, is already proving very tough competition for the high street lenders, and this trend is set to continue.

But where to obtain all this information? Many newspapers, including *The Sunday Times*, run regular articles on the best mortgage buys available, and give a weekly selection of the best rates on offer. For more detailed information, a monthly publication called *Moneyfacts* (see Appendix, page 134) lists all current mortgage offers. At the time of writing a single issue of the magazine costs £3.25 and, for those with access to a fax machine, it runs a daily updated information service on the best mortgage offers around.

Lack of information will not be a problem for the determined mortgage-hunter. The latest edition of *Moneyfacts* lists 95 'best buys' in its mortgage selection. Before making a choice, you should read the rest of this book first and think about the type of mortgage you want, and then start to examine the particular offers available.

2 | *The Step-by-Step Guide to House Purchase*

The whole process of buying a house or flat is almost inescapably lengthy, tedious and anxiety-inducing. True, there are folk tales – or perhaps urban myths – about the couple who walked into a house one day, exchanged contracts by the end of the week, and completed the sale a week after that. For most of us, it just isn't like that, but there is at least one consolation: the longer it takes, the longer you have to save up for all the expenses that will be incurred in the move. (For a detailed breakdown of these costs, see pages 27–31.)

There are a number of hoops that homebuyers are put through before purchasing a property. Because the legal system in Scotland is different (and, many believe, better) this guide only applies to house purchase in England, Wales and Northern Ireland. A separate section on Scotland follows (see page 27).

There is not much you can do to avoid moments of stress or exasperation in this business because many of the processes involved are outside your control. In fact, according to a professor of organizational psychology who has been researching the psychology of moving house, the 'golden rule' to limit the effects of stress is simply to accept that you are not in control. But you can at least arm yourself with knowledge of the way it all works, which should help.

Step 1: the groundwork
Well-prepared house-buyers will have undertaken some preliminary investigation even before they start house-hunting in earnest – looking around for mortgage offers, finding out how much they

can borrow, and saving enough cash for moving expenses and a decent deposit. If you are self-employed it would be wise to talk directly to a lender at this stage to find out how much, in principle, they are prepared to lend to you (see pages 5–9).

Step 2: the negotiation

You have found the house of your dreams: perhaps you are sitting with the owners in the living room, drinking a cup of their tea and nerving yourself to speak. Should you deal directly with them or make non-committal noises and talk to the estate agents later?

That is really up to you; there is no hard and fast rule. I have always conducted such negotiations face-to-face with the sellers and this has never been a problem. Others feel much happier conducting the negotiations at arm's length, through the agents. It might simply be a question of whether or not you like the individuals involved.

Should your initial offer be below the asking price? Here the answer is a definite yes. Occasionally one sees property advertisements stipulating 'no offers', but they are very rare these days. House prices are understood to be by negotiation, and you can always renegotiate upwards later, if necessary.

In any case, at this stage of the game any offer you make is not firm; it is conditional on the results of a valuation. A verbal offer should be followed up in writing, to the estate agents, and the magic formula you should add at the end goes: 'This offer is subject to valuation and survey, and subject to contract.' You may be asked at this stage to pay a small deposit – a matter of £100 or so – to the estate agent, as a sign of your serious intentions. This is returnable if the purchase does not go ahead.

Step 3: the survey and valuation

There may be some to-ing and fro-ing before this initial price is agreed, but you must then make a final decision on which mortgage lender you are going to use and provide all the details required, both on your income and the property concerned.

The lender's first job is to carry out a valuation on the property. This is purely for the benefit of the lender, not the borrower, but it is the borrower who pays for it. The cost is usually on a sliding scale according to the house value, although currently a few lenders are throwing in the valuation for free as part of their marketing package.

A valuation is just what it says: its purpose is to tell the lender what the house would probably sell for today. To establish that, some account has to be taken of the state of the place, but it will not be a detailed examination. If you want a proper report on the structure of the property you must go at least one step further. Most lenders these days operate a three-tier system. The cheapest option is the valuation; then there is a combined 'Homebuyer's Survey and Valuation' which includes a reasonably detailed report on the state of repair and general condition of the property; and finally, the full structural survey, which is the most expensive.

Table 2: Valuations and homebuyer's report

House price	Valuation	Homebuyer's report and valuation
£25,000	£130	£250
£50,000	£130	£250
£65,000	£150	£310
£80,000	£170	£325
£100,000	£170	£325
£150,000	£190	£375
£200,000	£220	£425

Source: Woolwich Building Society, 1995

Unless you are buying a brand-new home from a reputable builder, it would be wise to go at least for the second-tier homebuyer's survey rather than relying solely on the valuation. This report follows a basic format devised by the Royal Institution of Chartered Surveyors, and is described by the Woolwich Building Society as 'ideal for the average modern property'. Under its terms and conditions, surveyors undertake 'a visual inspection of so much of the exterior and interior of the property as is accessible with safety and without undue difficulty'.

So, for example, the surveyor will check for dampness within the property but will not move furniture or floor coverings, fixtures or fittings, and will look in the roof space but not examine individual timbers.

If you are buying a place that is in any way out of the ordinary, ancient, or even just old, there is a good case for having a full structural survey. There is, technically, a legal difference between a full structural survey and the other two types of report. While you pay for all three, it is only if you are commissioning a full structural survey that *you* become the surveyor's client; in the other two cases the client is the lender. So in theory, if things go wrong, you cannot sue the valuer because there is no contract between you. However, a number of recent court cases have established that surveyors do have some duty of care to the borrower as well as the lending institution.

While costs for the first two types of report are fixed by lenders, generally on a sliding scale according to the purchase price of the property, it is impossible to give exact costs for a full survey, because it will depend on the individual property, but Table 3 gives some 'typical' costs.

Table 3: The costs of a full survey: some typical examples

1930s 3-bed semi	£450–£550
Pre-1900s 4-bed detached	£550–£650
1970s 3-bed semi or terrace	£350–£450
1900s 3-bed semi or terrace	£500–£600

These costs include a valuation. VAT, currently at 17.5% would be payable in addition.

Source: Woolwich Building Society, 1995

Step 4:
If you are reasonably lucky, the first hiccup in the process may occur only at this stage: the valuation comes back at a lower price

than you have agreed to pay; or perhaps the structural survey is so full of horrors that you have serious doubts about whether it is a good idea to buy the place anyway.

A valuation below the agreed price is not the end of the world – indeed, it's almost inevitable. Valuers – and their employers, the mortgage lenders – are cautious people, particularly these days, and do not wish to be caught out by lending more than a property might fetch in a re-sale. If the discrepancy is no more than a thousand pounds or so, you may still be perfectly happy to go ahead with the purchase. You can, however, approach the sellers – or their estate agents – and make a new, lower offer on the basis of the valuation.

However, a valuation which is considerably lower than the agreed purchase price can cause serious problems. Lenders, you will remember, will only loan a percentage of the property price or valuation – *whichever is the lower*. In the worst instances, particularly if you were planning to borrow a very high percentage of the total, this may simply make the purchase impossible. And in many other cases, it you are borrowing more than 75% of the valuation, the loan will be more expensive because of the extra premium charged by lenders for a mortgage indemnity guarantee (see page 7). You might find you have to pay a higher interest rate as well.

So don't be afraid of going back to the sellers with a new, lower offer. Having checked what the extra costs of your loan will be, ask the sellers to reduce their price accordingly.

Bad news from a surveyor's report will almost certainly lead buyers to try to renegotiate the price, if they don't decide to abandon the purchase altogether. This is where a full structural survey can actually save buyers money; sellers may well be more willing to negotiate when faced with evidence, in black and white, of the extent of the problems with their property.

Step 5: the legal process

Once an offer has been agreed between buyer and seller, things can really get moving. You now need to instruct a solicitor to act on your behalf, and to get a firm offer of mortgage finance from a lender. For this you may need to produce employers' references, possibly bank references and, if self-employed, three years' accounts.

At this point, your offer is clearly no longer 'subject to survey' but it is still 'subject to contract', and either party can still pull out without penalty.

Expect the legal work to take months rather than weeks, even if there are no other complications down a house-buying chain. Among other things, this is what solicitors must do:

- Make sure the buyer will obtain vacant possession of the property
- Make enquiries as to whether there are any local developments in the pipeline which will affect the house or its value
- Advise on the draft contract for sale
- Examine the mortgage deed (the agreement between buyer and lender)
- Ensure the buyer obtains a proper title to the property (in other words, ensure it is really the seller's to sell)
- Examine the lease where the property is leasehold
- Arrange for any necessary registration of the title on behalf of the buyer.

There is also legal work to be undertaken on behalf of the lender; generally, one solicitor will act for both parties, buyer and lender, and the cost will be all-inclusive.

Step 6: the exchange of contracts
Once contracts have been exchanged between buyer and seller, both parties are committed to the deal. Completion traditionally takes place a month after exchange, though there is no legal requirement for this: it can be any length of time agreed by both parties.

At this stage buyers must put down a substantial deposit. A figure of 10% of the purchase price is the norm, but again, this is a matter for negotiation. A 5% deposit is reasonably common. Buyers – particularly first-time buyers – may want to pay as low a deposit as possible; sellers will hold out for more. If buyers pull out of the contract at this stage, they immediately forfeit the deposit, and can also be sued by the seller.

Once contracts are exchanged, the risk regarding the property passes to the buyers, who should make sure the property is properly insured – this is usually done by their solicitor.

Step 7: the completion
Congratulations: you've done it! On completion day, you get the keys and move in. The solicitor arranges for the mortgage money to be paid over to the seller, and from now on the place is yours.

Gazumping and Gazundering

Two unlovely words which describe what are, in my view, actions not far short of blackmail. Both are only possible because, under English law, there is such a long delay before both parties are legally committed to the deal.

Gazumping is more common when property prices are rising fast: it refers to the practice of sellers who, having accepted an offer from one purchaser, then accept a higher offer from someone else and tell the original buyer to match it or lose the property. Given that the original buyer may have already spent a large amount of money on legal work and surveys, it seems very unfair.

Gazundering is, if anything, even worse: it refers to buyers who, knowing their sellers are committed to the deal and have perhaps already arranged to buy another property on the back of it, drop their offer at the last minute by a few thousand pounds.

Neither action is illegal, and both reveal the shortcomings of the system. I can only hope that you never have the misfortune to enounter the sort of people who are prepared to do this.

Buying in Scotland

In Scotland an offer becomes binding to both parties at a much earlier stage. This means that more of the preparatory work has to be done before the offer is made.

So, once you have found a property you would like to buy, the first step is to arrange for a valuation and instruct a solicitor, who will write to his opposite number on the seller's side asking that his client's interest in the property is 'noted'. Before any offer is made a valuation (and, if required, a survey) must be carried out, and buyers must also get a firm offer of mortgage finance.

The procedure for making an offer is sometimes different in Scotland: instead of the seller nominating a price, and buyers coming in with lower offers, the seller may invite offers above a specified figure, known as the 'upset' price. It is then up to buyers to decide how much to offer, and to try to ascertain whether they are the only bidders or if they are in competition with others.

Once the offer is made and accepted through an exchange of letters between each party's solicitors, there is a firm contract between the two and the solicitor can proceed to transfer title and register it under the Land Register.

There are estate agents in Scotland, but it is more common to find solicitors' property centres which display details of large numbers of properties. Local newspapers are also a good source of information for the house-hunter.

The Costs of Buying and Selling

As Table 8 (see page 31) shows, the total costs of buying and selling are likely to amount to between £3,000 and £4,000. Some of the costs, such as valuation, stamp duty and land registry fees, vary according to the value of the property purchased. Estate agency fees – payable, of course, by the seller, not the buyer of a property – also depend directly on the selling price. They are typically between 1% and 2.5% for a sole agency, and a little more for a joint agency (see page 123).

Table 4: Land registry fees (cost of transferring title on previously registered property)

Cost of property	Transfers
up to £40,000	£40
£40,001–£60,000	£60
£60,001–£80,000	£80
£80,001–£100,000	£100
£100,001–£200,000	£150
£200,001–£500,000	£200
£500,001–£1,000,000	£500
£1,000,001 +	£1,000

Costs for first registration of title are higher. For example, £40 for property worth up to £25,000, £100 for property up to £60,000 and £200 for property up to £100,000.

Table 5: Stamp duty

Payable at 1% on full purchase price when this is above £60,000.

Solicitors and surveyors, by contrast, are more likely to charge according to the time taken. Conveyancing, in particular, is an enormously competitive field. Firms used to charge solely on the basis of a percentage of the property value, but these days they are more open to negotiation. Buyers should note, however, that the legal work for buying a flat may well be relatively more expensive

Table 6: Examples of legal costs

House price	Buying only	Buying and selling
£50,000	£298	£597
£65,000	£316	£637
£80,000	£336	£676
£100,000	£369	£742
£150,000	£437	£871
£200,000	£501	£1,007

Source: Woolwich Building Society, 1995

than for the purchase of a freehold house because going through a lease, for instance, involves more work.

Included in the solicitor's bill for purchase will be disbursements for local authority searches and the land registry fees and stamp duty. Thankfully, not all these costs have to be paid at once, but the bills do come thick and fast. Figure 2 shows the likely timetable for payment.

Figure 2: When do you usually pay?

Item	Before Offer	Before Exchange	Before Completion	1st Mortgage Payment
BUYING COSTS				
Reports and mortgage valuation	*			
Home Buyer's report	*			
Specialist reports	*			
Mortgage guarantee			*	
Stamp duty			*	
Searches			*	
Solicitor's fees			*	
Removal firm			*	
Building insurance				*
Deposit		*		
SELLING COSTS				
Solicitor's fees			*	
Estate agent's fees			*	

NB: Selling costs can be deducted from the proceeds of your sale.

Do remember that there may well be extra costs to be met at about the same time; they may include, for example:

- extra costs for fixtures and fittings
- premiums for buildings and contents insurance (see pages 118–21)
- transfer of telephone, gas and electricity (new telephone

subscribers may be asked to pay a deposit, and there will also be a charge if you are installing a line if there was not one there before)
- redirection of post
- the cost of a mortgage indemnity guarantee policy (see page 7)
- an administration fee on the mortgage (more common with fixed rate loans – see page 38).

At the time of writing many lenders are offering special deals, particularly to first-time buyers, to help with the cost of legal fees and the valuation. It is certainly worth keeping an eye out for such deals, but don't abandon your calculator. A saving of a few hundred pounds at the start could be paid for many times over if you are being offered a less than competitive mortgage rate.

Table 7a: Total costs of selling (average throughout England and Wales)

| | Sale price | | |
	£65,000	£80,000	£100,000
Solicitor	£321	£340	£373
Estate Agent	£1,633	£2,003	£2,449
Total	**£1,954**	**£2,343**	**£2,822**

Table 7b: Total costs of buying (average throughout England and Wales)

| | Purchase price | | |
	£65,000	£80,000	£100,000
Solicitor	£316	£336	£369
Land registry	£120	£140	£200
Searches	£70	£70	£70
Stamp duty	£650	£800	£1,000
Homebuyer's report	£310	£325	£325
Removals	£275	£315	£315
Total	**£1,741**	**£1,986**	**£2,279**

Source: Woolwich Building Society, 1995

Table 8: Typical costs by region (selling at £65,000; buying at £80,000)

East Anglia	£3,808
Greater London	£4,026
South-East	£3,958
Midlands	£3,291
North-East	£2,856
North-West	£2,794
Yorkshire	£3,000
South-West	£4,250
Wales	£3,486
Scotland	£3,707

Source: Woolwich Building Society, 1995

3 ‖ *Lenders and Interest Rates*

The Lenders: Who Are They?

Ten years ago, if you wanted a mortgage, you went to a building society. Today, a great many more institutions are eager to lend money for house purchase. They break down into three categories. First, there are still the building societies, who account for more than 60% of all the money lent on mortgages. Then there are the high street banks, who handle just under a third of all existing mortgages; and finally, a dozen or so 'specialist lenders' – a catch-all term for foreign-owned banks without a branch network in this country, other institutions which have concentrated on mortgage lending, and the 'direct' arms of a number of building societies and the like, where mortgage business is conducted over the telephone, for example, Direct Line and First Direct.

Most of the big newspapers carry details of mortgage 'best buys' every weekend, which is a good starting point for information, particularly with regard to the specialist lenders; mortgage brokers, too, should have information about the offers available from these lenders.

One point is worth bearing in mind if you choose a lender other than a building society or big bank. Traditionally, building societies have had a reasonably forbearing attitude to borrowers who get into difficulty with their repayments; some of the newer lenders have, in the past, been much tougher and quicker to institute repossession proceedings. In any case it should go without saying that if, at the outset, you are seriously worried you may not be able to keep up loan payments, you should think very carefully about whether it is wise to go ahead at all.

Interest Rates

Choosing the mortgage you take out to buy your home used to be a relatively simple matter: you had to decide whether to take out a repayment loan (see Chapter 4, page 44), or opt for an endowment or pension mortgage (see Chapter 5, page 55), but the actual business of choosing a loan was simple. You just looked at the rates on offer, and chose the cheapest.

Now all that has changed. At the time of writing you can take out a loan at a rate of anywhere between 1% and 9.99%. And which is a better deal – the 1% one? Not necessarily. In this particular case the special 1% offer was made to first-time buyers only and was restricted to loans of £150,000 or less. Most importantly, this rate only lasted for six months and then jumped to 6.54% for the succeeding six months; thereafter it was set to rise to the building society's ordinary variable rate which was 8.45% – compared with the then current basic rate of 8.35% charged by the biggest building societies, and around 7.4% charged by some specialist lenders. In addition, borrowers who took up the offer and then wanted to opt out during the first three years of the loan would have to pay a penalty of three months' interest.

So what about the 9.99% rate? That was on offer from a high street bank, as a fixed rate lasting from 1995 until either 2005, 2009, 2014 or 2019 – the borrower could choose. It carried a £250 administration fee, offered a £400 rebate, and charged a penalty of a full 12 months' interest if the loan was redeemed before the end of its fixed term.

So which loan *is* better? That has now become an extremely complicated question, and this case vividly illustrates how many factors come into play in making a choice. Borrowers need all their wits about them if they are to choose wisely.

Fixed or variable interest rate?

The first question borrowers should settle for themselves is whether they want a fixed or variable rate loan. Variable rates will move, by and large, in tandem with bank base rates, although the match is rarely exact either in timing or size. Bank base rates depend on the rate announced by the Chancellor and the Governor of the Bank of England. Their decision is influenced by a whole host of political and economic factors, in which you and I, as individual mortgage borrowers, feature as very small fry.

Building societies do not have to follow base rate movements exactly. Most of the money they raise to lend on to borrowers comes from individual savers. So if a society is getting plenty of money flowing in from savers, it may not have to raise its savings rates just because the base rate has risen. It may be able to hold off for a few weeks or even a few months; it may get away with a smaller rise than the base rate.

But on the other hand, if societies are having difficulty attracting money from savers – maybe because National Savings is competing too hard for that cash – then they may have to increase savings rates, which could take mortgage rates well above base rate; any drop in the base rate, however, may not be followed down all the way.

Overall, however, the two are tied together. Figure 3 shows the history of the two rates over the last 10 years.

It would seem logical to decide this question of fixed or variable rates on the basis of which will save you money in the long run. Unfortunately, this is just what you cannot do. No one can say for sure, or even with a small degree of certainty, that a fixed rate of, say, 8.5% over five years will turn out to cost borrowers more or less than a variable rate starting at 8.3%.

City analysts will often stick their necks out and attempt to predict the course of interest rates over the following 12 months, but even over this time span they apparently have a 50% chance at least of getting it wrong. There are very few predictions at all on where rates will go over longer periods.

There's an old joke about a stockbroker who answered his clients' questions about the direction of interest rates according to their name: those whose surnames began with the letters A to M were told rates were going up; those with names from the last half of the alphabet were told they were falling. 'That way,' observed the broker, 'at least I keep half my clients happy, even if I don't know which half.'

Figure 3: Interest rates: bank base rates versus mortgage rates

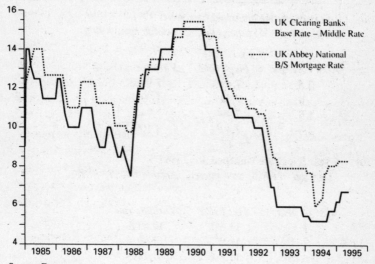

Source: Datastream

Table 9 gives examples, culled from the recent past, which illustrate how it is possible to get things satisfyingly right – or disastrously wrong. And each offer, at the time of launch, looked like a good buy.

While the two-year rate in this instance proved the clear winner against variable rates all the way through, the five-year rate rapidly became a loser – and although at the time of writing it has yet to run its full course, it looks as if the fixed rate borrower is certain to lose out overall.

Given that it is, to all intents and purposes, impossible to predict the direction of interest rates, borrowers must make their choice on other grounds. Mortgage brokers report that take-up on fixed rate mortgages soars during times when the fixed rate charged is lower than the current variable rate. This is understandable, on the 'bird in the hand' principle – at least borrowers know they will be saving money, if only in the short term; but even over relatively short terms, borrowers may still end up losing out.

Table 9: Fixed rate mortgages

(a) **2-year fixed rate launched November 1992**
Fixed rate: 7.49%; then current variable rate: 9.99%

	OUTCOME	
After — years	*Fixed rate*	*Variable rate*
0.5	7.49%	7.99%
1.0	7.49%	7.99%
1.5	7.49%	7.74%
2.0	7.49%	8.10%

(b) **5-year fixed rate launched June 1991**
Fixed rate: 11.8%; then current variable rate: 12.95%

	OUTCOME	
After — years	*Fixed rate*	*Variable rate*
1	11.8%	10.69%
2	11.8%	7.99%
3	11.8%	7.74%
4	11.8%	8.35%
5	11.8%	?

Source: National Westminster Bank p.l.c.

At the time of writing, some lenders are using very short-term fixed rates – up to two-year terms – as part of their package of what are, in effect, loss leaders to tempt in new mortgage customers. But for longer terms they have to 'match' their fixed rate loans with fixed rate assets, and that usually means going to the wholesale money markets, where the big financial institutions trade amongst themselves, and getting money there at the current rate. If they did not match their fixed rate loans in this way, they would be laying themselves open to the risk that interest rates would move up later, and they would be forced to pay more to their savers than they were getting in interest from their borrowers. This is precisely what the American equivalent of building societies, the Savings and Loans institutions, did some 10 years ago, and many of them effectively went bust as a result. They were saddled with lending money at fixed rates of maybe 5%, while finding they had to pay their savers more like 10% to attract their money.

So with these longer-term fixed rates (anything from three to 10 years), lenders can only offer what the market will let them. And the 'normal' situation is that long-term fixed rates are higher than variable rates. This is because savers are reluctant to lock up their money for long periods at a fixed rate unless they are offered some inducement to do so. Borrowers who want a long-term fixed rate on their mortgage should be prepared to pay a premium for the certainty that their borrowing costs won't rise. It is, if you like, an extra cost for a sort of insurance policy.

Although this is the 'normal' situation, there are still plenty of occasions when it may not apply, as table 9 shows. If everyone is confident that short-term interest rates are going to fall, quickly and sharply, then the long-term rate may actually be below the current variable rate. But, as the second example in Table 9 shows, even this situation won't guarantee that borrowers will profit from choosing the fixed rate.

Redemption penalties
All fixed rate offers carry early redemption penalties and, in theory at least, there is no way of escaping them, even if the lender would actually profit from an early opt-out. Typically, these penalties will be between three and 12 months' interest on the loan, although some lenders will work out sums individually for each borrower, depending on current interest rates.

Occasionally, it may be worth biting the bullet and paying a penalty to escape a very expensive fixed rate deal, but those times are few and far between, so don't go into a fixed rate deal on the basis that you can always escape later.

Fixed rate offers can disappear very quickly. Typically, a lender will arrange the savings side first, taking in a certain amount of money at such and such a rate for a predetermined period, and then make an offer to mortgage borrowers. Once the sum in question has been lent, the offer must be withdrawn, so borrowers will often have to make a snap decision. Here is a useful check-list of matters to look into before making that decision:

- **Level of fixed rate**: how does it compare with the current variable rate of that lender?
- **Length of term**: beware of short-term fixes; the associated costs (see below) can mean that what looks like a bargain deal turns out to be the opposite.
- **Lender's current basic variable rate**: at the end of the fixed term, borrowers may be obliged to go back on to the lender's variable rate; check to see how competitive this is with other major lenders.
- **Future fixed rate offers**: check whether the lender guarantees that a further fixed rate offer will be made when the original one runs out.
- **Redemption penalties**: all fixed rate loans carry penalties if they are redeemed before the end of the fixed rate term; a few may extend the penalties even beyond the end of the fixed term.
- **Portability**: the great majority of fixed rate loans are 'portable' – borrowers can carry on with them when they purchase a new property – but it is a point that should still be checked.
- **Application or administration fee**: a typical sum is £150 to £250. Check whether this is refundable if for any reason you do not take up the loan.
- **Method of repayment**: some fixed rate loans are only available on an endowment or pension basis (see Chapter 5, page 55).
- **'Compulsories'**: this is jargon in the mortgage trade for various types of insurance policy, which lenders sometimes

insist borrowers take out to qualify for some particular fixed rate offer. In some cases borrowers have to take out buildings and contents insurance through the lender concerned in order to be eligible for the loan, and this can work out more expensive than finding your own insurer (see Chapter 10, page 112). Other lenders will insist on borrowers taking out an insurance policy (again, through themselves) to cover mortgage payments in the event of sickness, accident or redundancy.

Table 10 details a fixed rate loan offer which was available during 1995, comparing it with one of the currently most competitive variable rates, and taking all the main factors into account. This exercise demonstrated to me how impossible it is to generalize: I chose to put my first-time buyer's house in a leafy suburb of a quiet country town; if I had placed it in the East End of London, it would have been a very different story. There, the insurance quotations from Direct Line – usually thought to be highly competitive – would actually have been more expensive than Yorkshire's. And if my buyer had managed on a 75% loan or less, there would have been no mortgage indemnity guarantee to pay on either side.

And the big (but inescapable) 'cheat' with this comparison is that I have assumed that both insurance premiums and variable mortgage rates will stay the same for the four years or so after the loan is taken out. Obviously they *will* change, but *how* they will change, both absolutely and in relation to each other, is anyone's guess.

Nevertheless, it is interesting to see how rapidly the apparent savings from a special offer can be overhauled by the longer-term savings on an 'ordinary' deal from competitive lenders. In this instance the variable rate deal is showing overall profits in a little under four years – but the fixed rate deal carries redemption penalties for borrowers who want to move their loan until the end of the fifth year.

This is not to say that my first-time buyer should automatically

Table 10: Fixed rate offer – comparing the cost

First time buyer borrowing £90,000 on £100,000 property in Worcester; interest only loan.

(a)   Fixed rate offer

- Fixed rate loan at 5.49%, fixed until 1.4.1997, from Yorkshire Building Society
- £250 administration fee
- Building and contents insurance must be taken out through lender
- Mortgage indemnity guarantee required for loans above 75%; rate for 90% borrowing: 7%
- Society's current basic variable rate: 8.44%.

(b)   Competing variable rate offer

- Variable rate loan currently at 7.39% from First Direct
- No administration fee and refund of valuation fee for first-time buyers
- Buildings and contents insurance not required through bank; policy arranged through Direct Line insurance
- Mortgage indemnity guarantee required for loans above 80%; rate for 90% borrowing: 6.66%.

Comparison of costs

From 1.6.1995 to 1.4.1997:

	Fixed rate	Variable rate
Monthly mortgage payments	£391.16	£526.53
Monthly insurance premiums	£33.66	£18.66
Total monthly costs over 22 months	£9,346.00	£11,994.18
(plus one-off costs):		
Mortgage indemnity guarantee	£1,050.00	£666.00
Administration fee	£250	
Less refund of valuation fee		−£170.00
Total costs over first 22 months	**£10,646.04**	**£12,490.18**
Following 2 years to 1.4.1999:		
Monthly mortgage costs	£601.35	£526.53
Monthly insurance costs	£33.66	£18.66
Total monthly costs over 24 months	**£15,240.08**	**£13,084.56**
Total (1.6.1995 to 1.4.1999)	**£25,886.12**	**£25,574.74**

have chosen the variable rate deal; he or she might decide rationally that the near-certainty of smaller savings in the first few years is preferable to the probability of larger savings later. In fact the only clear lesson to be learnt from the exercise is to look before you leap. Things are not, as you have probably already guessed, always quite so attractive as they seem!

There is one final point to bear in mind if you are choosing from a range of fixed rate offers: at the end of the fixed term you may be obliged to go back onto the lender's variable rate. Look back at Table 1 (page 10) to see the cost of loans at differing mortgage rates; if, after you have done your budgeting, you realize that there is no way you could afford payments at, for example, a 10% mortgage rate over the next three or four years, then it would be wiser to opt for a five-year fixed rate at 9% rather than the more alluring two-year fixed rate of 6%.

Caps and collars

Occasionally lenders offer a different type of loan, one where the interest rate is 'capped' – in other words, guaranteed not to rise above a certain rate for a fixed term. Occasionally this can be accompanied by a 'collar', which means the rate will not fall below some other specified rate. You might, for example, be offered a rate of 8% which is 'capped' for five years at 10% and 'collared' at 6% for the same period.

On the face of it, capped rates without a collar have advantages over fixed rates because if the general level of interest rates falls, borrowers can benefit from that – but they still have protection if rates rise. Whether this theory works in practice depends partly on the lenders' charging policy. If variable rates plummet, will borrowers on capped rates see theirs drop to the same extent, or can the lenders charge borrowers what they like, as long as it is below the cap? You will have to check this, but most lenders do bring their capped rate down to the same level as their variable rate.

Capped rate offers almost invariably carry an administration fee, which tends to be slightly higher than the equivalent for a fixed rate offer, so look closely at the term of the cap: if it only lasts for a year or so, it may hardly be worth your while buying it.

Discounts and cashbacks

In the last few years the proportion of borrowers taking out fixed or capped rate loans has soared. It has been anywhere between 40 and 60% of all new mortgages. However, building societies in particular need to lend most of their money at variable rates because the majority of their savings accounts are on that basis. To persuade borrowers to take out variable rate loans, lenders have come up with all sorts of special packages: short-term discounts off the variable rate, or big cashbacks for borrowers going onto the full variable rate from day one.

As with fixed rate offers, borrowers need to keep their eyes on a whole range of different factors when working out whether the offer is right for them: How long does the discount last? What are the redemption penalties, and how long do they last? (Don't assume the two periods will be identical. Typically, you may find that an offer of a discount lasting for three years has attached to it redemption penalties lasting for six years.) Does the offer require the borrower to take out buildings insurance through the lender and, if so, how expensive is it compared with other policies? Do lenders impose a maximum on the percentage of the property value they will lend? Although lenders' usual maximum may be 95%, they may impose a lower figure on certain discount offers, perhaps as low as 70%, which may well put them out of reach of first-time, and perhaps many second-time buyers.

Interest rates: 'flat' rates versus APRs

The Annual Percentage Rate (APR) is a legally defined system for working out interest rates devised to take the legwork out of comparing loan offers by automatically including the cost of all the 'strings' attached to any particular deal. With regard to mortgages, an APR must take account of the costs attached to the loan, such as a valuation fee, redemption penalties, administration fee, mortgage indemnity policy and insurance premiums, if these are a condition of the loan.

In practice, APRs don't help. Most borrowers need buildings insurance anyway; a compulsory policy only becomes an issue if it is more expensive than the alternatives. Then there are problems with other costs: the impact of flat charges, such as an administration fee, on the overall cost of the loan will vary according to the size of the loan. And with short-term fixed rate loans, the picture becomes yet murkier; lenders have to quote an APR for the full term of the loan even if the fixed rate term only lasts a few years. So, while lenders are obliged by law to quote APRs, borrowers should pay little, if any, attention to them.

4 | *Repayment Mortgages*

As a borrower, you have two basic options when it comes to repaying the loan. Either you can pay the borrowed capital back as you go along, or you can choose to pay only interest on the loan and, at the same time, start some form of regular savings which should, over the years, grow and enable you to repay all the capital in one go at the end of the term – and perhaps even provide a surplus as well.

There are pros and cons on each side. What is often ignored in all the debate about which is better is the fact that they are not necessarily mutually exclusive. For some reason, in their minds people tend to put their various financial affairs into watertight compartments – this is my mortgage, that's my savings, this other thing is my pension – but they all belong to the same person and ideally, in financial planning, you should think about the whole, not the separate parts.

If you have a repayment mortgage, for instance, you may still have a regular savings scheme which you can use to pay off all or part of the mortgage early; similarly, if you have an endowment or a Pep mortgage, there is nothing to stop you paying back capital on a regular or occasional basis whenever you have cash to spare.

Nevertheless, you must make an initial decision on how your loan is to be set up. In this chapter we concentrate on repayment mortgages; in Chapter 5 we will deal with the various types of interest-only mortgages linked to savings schemes, such as endowments, Peps, and pension plans.

Repayment Mortgages: How They Work

The repayment basis is in many ways the simplest and most obvious method of paying back a mortgage. Capital is paid back gradually every month and at the end of the chosen term, so long as borrowers have not fallen behind on their payments, the loan is guaranteed to be paid off.

If interest rates remain the same for the term of the loan, the monthly payment also stays the same. This may seem obvious, but in fact a certain amount of juggling behind the scenes is needed to arrange this. As the amount of capital repaid grows, so the interest on the outstanding amount falls – so how is it that the monthly payments stay level? Shouldn't they go down? The answer is no, because that is all taken into account before the payments are worked out. At the start of a mortgage each monthly payment consists almost entirely of interest and scarcely any capital is repaid.

Many first-time borrowers find their first annual mortgage statement a matter for outrage, if not despair. Having worked hard to make all their mortgage payments, they often find that the amount of capital owed has not decreased one iota; indeed, it may even have increased by a small amount. This is thanks to the fact that the amount of capital they have actually repaid during the year is tiny, and the interest due for the coming year is then loaded onto the total for that year. (Not all lenders work out mortgage repayments in exactly the same way, but all the building societies use this method.)

The proportion of capital repayment within each monthly payment grows steadily over the years, and during the last few years of the term the payments consist largely of capital rather than interest. Table 11 shows how much capital is repaid after various time periods, assuming a standard 25-year loan, and assuming that the current mortgage rate remains constant throughout the term.

After five years, when borrowers are a fifth of the way through their term, less than a tenth of the capital has been repaid – 7.7%

Table 11: Capital repayments on a £60,000 mortgage over 25 years

End of year	Capital repaid during year	Total repaid
1	£785	£785
2	£852	£1,637
3	£923	£2,560
4	£1,001	£3,561
5	£1,086	£4,647
6	£1,178	£5,825
7	£1,277	£7,102
8	£1,385	£8,487
9	£1,502	£9,989
10	£1,628	£11,617
15	£2,442	£22,068
20	£3,609	£37,676
25	£5,104	£60,000

Rate of interest assumed: 8.44%.

Source: Nationwide Building Society

to be precise, although this proportion changes slightly depending on the level of interest rates. Higher interest rates mean capital is paid back even more slowly; lower rates will speed up the process.

This is an important point to bear in mind if you anticipate moving within five years or so. You will not have repaid much capital during that time, but at least you will have paid something back, which is not the case with the other types of loan.

Length of term

Mortgages are almost always set up to run for 25 years, at least for borrowers under the age of 40 or thereabouts. If you are over 40 lenders may prefer to impose a shorter time frame, so that the final repayment is completed by the time you retire.

Negotiating a shorter time-span is never a problem; if you are under 35 at the outset, you are unlikely to be refused a longer term, although 30 years is probably the sensible limit. Shorter-term mortgages are initially more expensive, but save money over the longer term. Table 12 gives some examples both of monthly costs and total costs over the term.

Table 12: Repayment mortgages – different terms

Assuming a £60,000 mortgage at an interest rate of 8.44%

Term (years)	Monthly payments	Capital repaid after — years				Total Cost
		5	10	15	20	
25	£456	£4,647	£11,617	£22,068	£37,676	**£136,737**
20	£496	£7,522	£18,800	£35,716	£60,000	**£119,102**
15	£571	£12,818	£32,038	£60,000	n.a.	**£102,749**
10	£732	£24,236	£60,000	n.a.	n.a.	**£87,779**

Source: Nationwide Building Society

On the face of it, it looks as if you could save almost £50,000 in total by choosing a 10-year term rather than a 25-year term. But while these figures seem very precise, they should be viewed with a degree of scepticism. The biggest unknown is what inflation is going to do over the next quarter of a century; if we go through another period of high inflation at some point, the eventual savings achieved by choosing a shorter-term loan may be worth (in today's terms) very little, but the repayments must be made in 'good' money today.

In any case, as interest rates move (which they undoubtedly will, both up and down during this period) the calculations will change, and so too, will the total amount saved.

Nevertheless, you can still apply a test by asking yourself the question: what would I be doing with the extra money saved by opting, say, for a 25-year mortgage term rather than a 20-year one? If I invested it, would it earn a return equal to the mortgage interest rate I am paying? If the answer is no – and if, of course, you can afford it – it may be sensible to choose a shorter term.

One aspect of these tables may look curious to those who are not mathematicians. Moving from a 25- to a 20-year term means paying an extra £40 a month; but to 'save' a further five years and drop down to a 15-year term involves a much larger extra payment – £75 in this case – while the difference between the 15-year and 10-year monthly payments is much larger still.

For many borrowers a 15- or 10-year mortgage term will be out of the question: it is just too expensive. If they could afford it, in all likelihood they would prefer to borrow a larger capital sum over a longer term, and thus buy a nicer house. But the difference between 20 and 25 years is relatively small, and these days I advise all new borrowers to consider the 20-year option alongside the 25-year one. For a little extra each month they will be paying capital back much faster and, of course, getting five 'free' years at the end of the term.

What if interest rates rise? Oddly enough, the higher interest rates are, the smaller the difference between a 20- and 25-year loan. With a mortgage rate of 15%, for example, the difference is not £40 per month, but something under £30.

Another approach is to consider adapting the term to your changing lifestyle. A couple buying today, with two full-time salaries coming in, could start out on a 20-year loan, thus accelerating the speed at which they pay back capital. Then, when they have children and the family is down to one regular salary, they could apply to extend the term of the loan, cutting down the monthly payments. And later, when both partners are back at work they could speed the process up again.

Table 13 shows how this might work in practice.

Many people don't realize that they can adjust their repayment term like this, but flexibility is one of the great advantages of repayment mortgages and more borrowers could reap the benefits. What is more, lenders do not, at the time of writing, make a charge for arranging these adjustments. However, if you are planning to extend the term rather than reduce it, you must get formal permission from the lender first. Unless you have failed to keep up your payments, you should not encounter any problems, but taking unilateral action would mean that, technically, you end up in arrears, which is tedious, and possibly expensive, to sort out.

Occasional repayments

Borrowers can make extra capital repayments at any time, but it is worth checking with your lender first to see what rules there are on this. Most building societies stipulate a minimum sum before they will make an immediate adjustment to the loan. This is usually either a flat sum – £250 to £1,000 is typical – or a number of monthly payments, perhaps three or four.

Table 13: How to adjust your repayment mortgage

In January 1995 John and Jane were both earning £20,000 a year. They took out a £60,000 repayment mortgage. Because they could easily afford it, they chose a 20-year term. In January 2000 Jane has a child and gives up work. With the family down to one income they reschedule the mortgage to last for a fresh 25-year term.

Five years later, in January 2005, Jane goes back to work on a part-time consultancy basis; John, meanwhile, has had a couple of promotions. Although they are now saving for school fees, they still have money to spare. They choose to reschedule the remaining loan over 15 years, bringing its completion date to 2020 – 25 years after they took it out.

Date	Loan outstanding	Term (years)	Monthly payments
1.1.95	£60,000	20	£496.26
1.1.00	£52,478	25	£395.20
1.1.05	£48,377	15	£455.72
1.1.20	nil		

In January 2005 John and Jane could decide instead to reschedule the mortgage over just 10 years rather than 15. This would increase their monthly payments to £585.76 rather than £455.72, and the loan would be repaid in full in January 2015, exactly 20 years after they took it out.

Interest rate assumed: 8.44% throughout.

Source: Nationwide Building Society

You can pay smaller amounts at any time, but they will not be credited until the end of the society's financial year. In theory, therefore, it is wise to tuck away such sums into an interest-bearing account until that time. Most societies have a year-end coinciding with the calendar year, but do check. Other lenders, including most of the banks, will accept any sum at any time and credit it to your account immediately.

Table 14 shows the long-term effect of making occasional lump-sum repayments.

Table 14: Effect of making additional capital repayments

Jim has a £60,000 repayment mortgage set up to last for 25 years. He gets a Christmas bonus each year of £1,000. With great financial acumen – and even greater self-control – he uses it to pay off part of his mortgage, meanwhile keeping monthly payments at the previous level. After five years of this self-denial the end result, at least, is pleasing.

	With no extra repayments	With 5 × £1,000 annual repayments
Monthly payments (years 1–5)	£455.79	£455.79
Capital repaid (after five years)	£4,648	£10,566
Mortgage repaid after	25 years	20 years 8 months
Total cost	£136,737	£112,813

Total savings: £23,924

Source: Nationwide Building Society

What all these examples illustrate, in essence, is the effect of compound interest. From time to time publications appear which promise to reveal 'special ways to slash mortgage costs' – but there are no special ways, only the simple matter of paying back more capital, and more frequently, than you are obliged to.

Repayment mortgages and fixed rates

Borrowers who opt for fixed rate loans or special discounted rates do have to be careful, however, if they intend to pay off extra sums at any time. Both these types of loan carry early redemption penalties which run for a predetermined period, and any extra capital payment made will trigger them off.

In this case, one option would be to start saving in a Tessa – a Tax Exempt Special Savings Account; these are offered by all building societies and banks. They must run for five years and, so long as the conditions are adhered to, the interest is tax free. Tessas have a maximum overall savings limit of £9,000, of which no more than £3,000 may be invested in the first year and up to £1,800 in each subsequent year. At the end of the term, assuming the redemption penalties on the loan have ceased to apply, the proceeds can be used to pay down the mortgage.

Repayment mortgages and moving

One of the perceived drawbacks of repayment mortgages is that every time you move you have to start all over again; with an endowment or Pep type of mortgage, it is claimed, you have at least accumulated a fair-sized sum in the savings plan.

This criticism is based largely on a misunderstanding. It is true that, until they reach a certain age, borrowers *can*, if they wish, take out fresh 25-year mortgages every time they move, which obviously has the effect of pushing back the date of final repayment yet further into the future. But they don't *have* to: it makes more sense to take out a mortgage with a shorter time-span on each move. The two examples in Table 15 illustrate how this could work in practice. In each case, for the sake of transparency, we have assumed that the borrower is not 'trading up' or borrowing more each time he or she moves. It has also been assumed that interest rates remain constant at 8.44%. Different interest rates will produce slightly different figures, but the principle remains the same.

Table 15: Moving house with a repayment mortgage

Example (a):
Borrower takes out a £60,000, 25-year repayment
mortgage and moves after 5 years.

Loan 1

Capital outstanding at start of term	£60,000
Monthly repayments on 25-year loan	£455.79
Capital outstanding at end of year 5	£55,352

Loan 2

Capital oustanding at start of term		£55,352
Monthly repayments on		
	25-year loan	£418.34
	20-year loan	£455.79
	15-year loan	£524.72

Example (b):
Borrower takes out £60,000, 25-year repayment
mortgage and moves after 10 years.

Loan 1

Capital outstanding at start of term	£60,000
Monthly repayments on 25-year loan	£455.79
Capital outstanding at end of year 10	£48,384

Loan 2

Capital oustanding at start of term		£48,384
Monthly repayments on		
	25-year loan	£362.31
	20-year loan	£395.27
	15-year loan	£455.79
	10-year loan	£585.85

Note: assumes mortgage interest rate of 8.44%.

Source: Nationwide Building Society

As this table indicates, the monthly payments for loan (2) are
identical to those for loan (1) when the overall term (for the two
loans) adds up to 25 years.

Repayment mortgages and mortgage indemnity guarantees

The mortgage indemnity guarantee (MIG) is an insurance policy which the lender takes out in cases where borrowers are borrowing (generally) more than 75% of the valuation of their property. The cost of the policy is paid by the borrower, either directly or disguised as an extra fee for high percentage lending.

The costs of these policies are given in more detail in Chapter 7 (page 81), but it is worth noting here that repayment mortgages can help to cut the cost on a subsequent move. A borrower who takes out a 95% endowment-type mortgage today and moves after five years would need to see house prices rise by approximately 28% in order to escape an MIG charge completely on his next property. If he takes out a repayment mortgage, however, thanks to the capital paid back, house prices need only rise by 20% to free him from the MIG requirement on the move.

Life assurance

If you die within the term of a repayment mortgage, there will be a large debt to repay. It is sensible, therefore, to take out some form of life assurance, especially if you have dependants. A particular type of policy, known as a Decreasing Term Assurance or a Mortgage Protection Policy, is tailor-made for this situation. Under this policy, the sum assured – the amount payable on death – declines each year, to match the decreasing amount of capital still outstanding.

Because the life assurance company's possible exposure is falling with each year you stay alive (and pay back more capital), the premiums are lower than they would be with an ordinary term assurance policy, which pays out a fixed sum on death within the term.

This type of policy may or may not be appropriate for you – it depends on your full personal circumstances – but if you are comparing the costs of the various methods of mortgage payment, then this is the very minimum protection needed by anyone with a repayment mortgage. (For a more detailed discussion of life assurance, see Chapter 10, page 112.)

Repayment mortgages: the end of the term

One question that new borrowers should keep in the back of their minds is what they will do when they are close to the end of the mortgage term – after year 20, for example, of a 25-year loan.

Building societies, and some other lenders, calculate the interest due by taking the amount of capital outstanding at the beginning of a year, and working out the interest due on that sum, which is then paid in instalments each month.

It has already been noted that, as the end of the term approaches, the proportion of the monthly payment representing capital repaid grows. What this means, in practice, is that the effective rate of interest paid by the borrower rises. One or two years before the end of the mortgage term, therefore, it will pay to raid your savings and pay off the outstanding balance early.

5 | *Endowments, Peps and Pension Mortgages*

Around seven out of 10 borrowers are now buying their homes with an endowment, Pep or pension mortgage. All three schemes work on the same basic principle: instead of paying off capital as you go, you pay only interest throughout the full term of the loan, and the entire capital sum is then paid off in one go from the proceeds of a savings scheme taken out at the start of the mortgage.

Inevitably, there's a lot of information that needs to be absorbed if borrowers are to understand exactly what these schemes offer. And it could turn out to be a waste of time if, in the end, you decide on a repayment mortgage. So readers who merely want a summary of the pros and cons of different types of mortgage are quite welcome to skip this chapter and go onto the next.

Mortgages that use an endowment policy for building up savings are the most popular of all these products. They are currently chosen by nearly six out of 10 borrowers. A further one in 10 borrowers chooses a Personal Equity Plan (Pep) or a pension plan. These three financial animals are different in many respects – the tax treatment of their underlying investments, for example – but essentially they all put people's savings into equities (company shares) which should, over the long term, prove a rewarding investment. But they do need to be examined in more detail.

Endowment Mortgages

Endowment mortgages are a package deal. Part of each monthly payment goes to pay for straightforward life assurance, so if the borrower dies before the end of the term the mortgage will be paid off. The rest – the larger portion of the payment – goes into a life assurance-linked savings policy, which is usually invested by the lender in a mixture of company shares, commercial property, and some government securities ('gilts').

How the premiums are calculated

The monthly payments are set according to three main factors: firstly, of course, the size of the loan to be paid off at the end of the term; secondly the length of the term; and thirdly the age and sex of the borrower – and usually some additional health factors such as whether he or she is a smoker or not.

The older borrowers are when they take out the loan, the higher the monthly payments will be. This is because, statistically speaking, they are more likely to die before the end of the term, in which case the life company will have to pay up extra to meet its guarantee. If borrowers have a history of bad health they may be asked to have a medical examination before the life company takes them on, but that is extremely rare for anyone under 40.

Table 16 gives some examples of the monthly premiums currently required to pay off a mortgage of £60,000. If a couple is buying a house together, the usual practice is to organize the policy on a 'joint lives, first death' basis. This means that if either one dies before the end of the term, the loan will automatically be paid off.

The key thing to remember with endowment mortgages is that they guarantee to pay off the loan in full only if you die before the end of the term. Otherwise you are guaranteed only that a certain minimum figure will be paid out when the policy matures. This minimum is usually roughly equal to the total of all the premiums paid during the term.

Assuming you survive the full term, there ought to be enough to pay off the loan, but it will all depend on whether the life company's investments have performed at least as well as they were expected to. And how well is that, precisely? This is one of the pieces of information that you will be given, but it will come along with a mass of other stuff, so look out for it.

Table 16: Monthly cost of £60,000 endowment mortgage

Borrower	Endowment + premium	interest	= Total monthly payments	Term of loan (years)
Man aged 25	£98.28	+ £386.10	= £484.38	25
Man aged 30	£99.63	+ £386.10	= £485.73	25
Man aged 35	£102.40	+ £386.10	= £488.50	25
Woman aged 25	£97.56	+ £386.10	= £483.66	25
Woman aged 30	£98.64	+ £386.10	= £484.74	25
Woman aged 35	£100.40	+ £386.10	= £486.50	25
Joint Lives				
Man 40, Woman 38	£114.07	+ £386.10	= £500.17	25
Man 45, Woman 43	£167.20	+ £386.10	= £553.30	20
Man 50, Woman 48	£258.40	+ £386.10	= £644.50	15

These days new endowment mortgages are usually set up on the assumption that investments are going to grow by either 7 or 7.5% a year. Some years ago people were more optimistic about investment returns, and anything up to 8.5 or even 9% was assumed. The assumed growth rate is crucial, because it could dictate whether or not there is enough in the kitty to pay off the loan at the end of the term.

Table 17 shows the annual returns achieved with endowment policies that have matured in the past few years.

Looking only at the 25-year figures is highly reassuring, but could be misleading. Those policies were started back in the late 1960s or 1970, and worked their way through a period of high

Table 17: Past results of with-profit endowment policies

Maturing in Year	25-YEAR POLICIES			10-YEAR POLICIES		
	Lowest	Average	Highest	Lowest	Average	Highest
1993	11.0%	12.6%	13.6%	6.5%	11.4%	13.7%
1994	11.1%	12.8%	13.9%	8.2%	10.9%	13.3%
1995	10.9%	12.7%	13.6%	7.3%	10.0%	12.4%

Source: Money Marketing/Alexander Clay & Partners

inflation and high levels of investment return. All investment experts are agreed that with much lower inflation today, investment returns are also likely to be lower for the forseeable future.

Nevertheless, an annual growth rate of 7.5% seems a reasonable guess for future returns. But borrowers don't have to take anyone's word for it: if they prefer to opt for a lower investment return, they can do so, although most lenders do not volunteer that information; this may well offer better value for money for those who can afford it.

Of course, the lower the investment growth rate you assume for your policy, the higher the monthly premiums to pay back a loan. To take one example, the monthly premiums for a man aged 30 taking out a 25-year £60,000 mortgage work out at £99.63 a month if a growth rate of 7% is assumed. But on a growth rate of just 5%, the monthly premiums must rise to £130.13.

So what does the borrower get for the extra money? Added security, of course, so that if investment returns are less than expected, his loan may still be paid off in full. And if the returns do turn out to be higher, there will be a surplus after paying back the loan. In this example, assuming the investment return turns out to be 7.5% a year, the policy would produce £76,200 at the end of the term, leaving £26,200 for the borrower's own use after paying back the mortgage.

In fact, the type of endowment policy used for mortgage purposes today does carry some sort of guarantee that there will be sufficient to pay off the loan: the life company monitors the progress of the investments and if, after a few years, it looks as if the target growth rate is going to be missed, it tells policyholders to increase their premiums. Generally speaking, life companies will carry out their first review at year 10 of a 25-year policy, then again at year 15, year 20, and possibly annually thereafter.

With-profits endowment policies

The most common form of policy used for an endowment mortgage is a with-profits policy. The premiums are invested in a large fund which has a massive spread of investments. The lion's share is likely to be in British and foreign company shares – typically between 60 and 70% of the total – with perhaps 15 or 20% in commercial property and the remainder in fixed interest securities.

Investment returns are allocated to individual policies in two ways. Each year, an annual bonus is declared by the life company. This is likely to be a figure in the region of 6 or 7% and it is added to the total of the premiums already paid into the policy. Once this bonus is added, it cannot be taken away, so in effect the guaranteed sum grows gradually each year.

The annual bonus, broadly speaking, represents the income earned by the life company's investments each year. The terminal bonus is applied to an individual policy just once – as its name implies, right at the end of the term. Roughly speaking, this represents the capital growth achieved by the investments over the full term of the policy.

Bonus levels of each type are decided by the life company's actuary, who has some leeway in making his decision. The idea of a with-profits policy is to smooth out investment returns from one year to the next, and to do this the life company needs to carry reserves, which it can dip into if investment returns in any year have been particularly bad, or add to if they are better than expected. This feature makes with-profits policies less risky than other types of equity investment, although they are not risk-free.

It should be noted that the above method of allocating bonuses relates to what are called 'unitized with-profits contracts'. This is the type of policy almost universally on sale today. If you have a with-profits policy that was started some years ago, it is likely to be what is now called a 'conventional with-profits contract'; here, the procedure for allocating annual bonuses is slightly different.

Policyholders start with a 'guaranteed sum assured', pretty much a notional figure which represents the guaranteed death benefit under the policy before it is topped up with extra term assurance to reach the mortgage figure. Annual bonuses are then declared at a much lower rate – currently around 3 to 4% – but because the guaranteed sum assured is much higher than the total premiums paid in the early years, it is very similar in effect to the higher annual bonuses declared on unitized contracts.

In fact, whether the policy is 'unitized' or 'conventional' should in itself make no difference to the results at the end of the policy's term; it is largely a matter of terminology.

Unit-linked endowment policies

With a unit-linked endowment policy the investor gets what's coming to him directly. Policyholders are allocated units representing their share of an underlying investment fund. If the fund does well, policyholders get the full benefit; if badly, the full damage.

Unit-linked policies offer a choice of specialist funds, of which the most commonly chosen for mortgage purposes is a 'managed fund', investing in a similar spread of investments to a with-profits policy. But it is possible to choose, for example, a UK equity fund, a property fund, or one investing solely in international equities.

Generally speaking, unit-linked policies are not used much for endowment mortgages, but they exist for anyone who might want them.

Life policies and tax

Policyholders do not have to pay any tax on the proceeds of life assurance policies, but this does not mean the investments themselves are totally 'tax-free'. The life company is responsible for paying tax on the income and any capital gains realized within its funds, and this is deducted from the funds' value each year.

What this means in effect is that life company investments can be expected to grow at a slower rate than a totally tax-free investment such as a Pep. For mortgage purposes, while a growth rate of 7.5% is assumed for endowment policies, Peps are generally expected to grow at 9% a year. This difference reflects the impact of tax.

One last point to note: while basic rate taxpayers never face any extra tax charge on the proceeds of life policies (whether they wait until maturity date or cash the policy in early), higher rate taxpayers could face an extra charge – at a rate representing the difference between basic and higher rate tax – if they cash in the policy before the end of the term.

Cashing-in early

'Early surrender' of life policies is not a good idea in any case. This is because a lot of the expenses of running a life policy are taken out in the early years of a policy's life, and if you were to cash in after just a couple of years or so, you would be highly unlikely to get back as much money as you had paid in.

These days life companies have to be very explicit about charges in the detailed illustrations they issue to potential policyholders, and these must include the effect of early surrender. As a rough rule-of-thumb, on a 25-year policy – unless the investment performance is way above expectations – you would be unlikely to get back the full amount of premiums paid until the policy had been in force for a good four years, and you would have to wait much longer before it started to achieve a decent return.

With-profits policies can carry a further sting in their tail when it comes to cashing in early. Much of the overall return on a maturing policy comes from the terminal bonus, which is added right at the end of the policy's life. These days the terminal bonus typically accounts for at least half the total return on 25-year policies. If you cash in early, you may get no terminal bonus at all; it is in any case likely to be less than your 'fair share'.

This may depend on whether you have the (modern) unitized with-profits policy or the (old-fashioned) conventional policy. Unitized policies tend to be more generous and give all policyholders a fair share of the terminal bonus even if they cash in early; conventional policies often impose penalties.

Pep Mortgages

Pep mortgages work on the same basis as endowments, and they are steadily becoming more popular. Personal Equity Plans were devised to encourage investors to put their money into British company shares, but over the years they have been allowed to invest more widely. A maximum of £6,000 can be put into a Pep each year; at least 50% of each plan must be invested in UK or European Community shares – the rest can be in fixed interest securities or shares from other parts of the world.

Peps for mortgages are usually unit trust or investment trust Peps. These two vehicles are pooled investments, giving small investors exposure to a much greater number of individual shares – typically between 40 and 100 – than they could achieve by buying shares themselves.

The big attraction of Peps is that they are totally tax-free; as long as the rules are obeyed, there is no income tax to pay on the dividends and no capital gains tax on the growth. So, in theory, 'pepped' investments should grow faster than a life company fund, and it is therefore reasonable to assume a higher growth rate when calculating the monthly sum required to pay off a mortgage.

Peps have another advantage over endowments: they are much more flexible. Within the overall £6,000 limit, investors can usually increase or decrease their monthly savings without penalties, and they can cash in the plan at any time without penalties. Naturally, if you are saving with a view to paying off the mortgage, this would not be sensible. But suppose the investments grow at a much faster rate than expected; at year 18, for example, perhaps you have already accumulated enough to repay the loan. With a Pep, this is no problem. With an endowment policy, you could still lose out thanks to surrender penalties.

Peps and life assurance

Peps do not, however, provide any life assurance cover themselves. If you need such cover, it will have to be paid for separately. This is a point to remember when comparing costs.

Pep mortgages: the costs

Table 18 gives some indication of the current costs of a Pep mortgage. They are worked out on the assumption that the underlying investments will grow by 9% a year.

Table 18: Monthly cost of a £60,000 Pep mortgage

Pep investment	Mortgage + interest	Cost excluding = life assurance	Life + assurance	= Total	Term of loan
£76.63	+ £386.10	= £462.73	+ £13.00	= £475.73	25 years
£119.78	+ £386.10	= £505.88	+ £47.00	= £552.88	20 years
£197.80	+ £386.10	= £552.88	+ £62.00	= £614.88	15 years

Source: London & Country Mortgages, Perpetual Investment Management

The life assurance policy used in these examples is level term assurance (see page 115), which pays out the full £60,000 on death within the term, irrespective of how much the Pep investments have grown. Given the volatility of equity markets and the fact that Pep investments will rise or fall according to the stockmarket, this is usually considered a more sensible choice than a decreasing term assurance (see page 113). In these examples the premium for the 25-year loan is based on a man aged 30; for the 20-year loan, on a couple aged 45 and 43; and for the 15-year loan, on a couple aged 50 and 48.

Borrowers can choose to assume that their Pep will grow at a faster or slower rate than the 9% used here, but most lenders would be reluctant to accept a higher figure (though they may be happy to lend on an interest-only basis – see page 66). Table 19 shows the level of regular savings required with a Pep if different rates are chosen.

Pension Mortgages

For many people, their pension plan represents the largest part of their savings, and in theory there is no reason why they cannot link repayment of their mortgage to the pension.

The rules and regulations regarding pensions are extremely complex, but whatever sort of pension you have – whether it is a personal pension, or one of a variety of company pension schemes – the rules allow you to take a large chunk of the proceeds as a tax-free cash sum on retirement. With personal pensions the basic rule is that you can take up to a quarter of the total pension fund as cash; with company schemes, rules are more complicated and depend in part on how long you have worked for the company concerned.

Table 19: Pep mortgages – monthly savings needed to produce capital sum of £60,000

Investment rate p.a.	Term of loan (years)	Monthly savings
6%	25	£117.85
12%	25	£48.76
6%	20	£166.99
12%	20	£84.76
6%	15	£251.46
12%	15	£154.55

Source: Perpetual

Pension investments, like Peps, grow tax-free, making them a very tax-efficient form of saving. And, better than Peps, pension premiums are fully tax-deductible, so that a £1,000 investment effectively costs a basic rate taxpayer £750 (£760 from April 96), and a higher rate taxpayer £600. But there are many reasons why linking mortgage repayment to a pension is not a good idea.

For example, borrowers under 40 taking out a pension mortgage may be committing themselves to a much longer term than the normal 25 years because they can only get the tax-free cash at retirement. In addition, it is fair to say that most people do not save as much as they should in pension plans in any case, and imposing the additional burden of mortgage repayment on the scheme could make the difference between an adequate income in old age, and poverty.

Another potential drawback is that the amount of money people are allowed to save in a pension each year is limited by law.

So even if they wanted to increase their pension savings to make up for the mortgage cost, they could be constrained by these rules.

Finally, employment patterns have been changing over the last few years; people can no longer predict with certainty that they are going to be in the same job, or even the same sort of job, for the rest of their normal working lives. In the future employees may well become self-employed, or vice versa; that could mean having to change pension plans, thus messing up their mortgage arrangements. And being forced to take early retirement – a common enough occurrence these days – can be very awkward if you have the mortgage tied up with your pension.

That said, there may be individual circumstances where a pension mortgage is a good idea. If you are attracted by the idea it would be wise to talk it over with a professional financial adviser or accountant before going ahead.

Another point to bear in mind is that, at first sight, the pension mortgage appears to be the most expensive option of all. This is because the pension premiums have to grow into a fund approximately four times the size of the mortgage so that you can withdraw 25% as a cash sum to repay the loan. Some examples are given in Table 20.

One last point: Table 20b should be viewed with a healthy dose of scepticism. In the first place, the size of the accumulated fund will depend entirely on how the investments grow during the term. While this table assumes a rate of 9%, there is no knowing what it might actually be. And the size of the annual pension remaining, after borrowers have taken their 25% as a cash lump sum, will itself depend on the level of interest rates at the time they retire. The figures in the table assume the interest rate will be 7.5%, but it could be either higher or lower.

Finally, of course, do remember that inflation in the intervening years could wreak havoc with the real value of that pension. Don't make the mistake of thinking that just because you have a pension mortgage, you have automatically made all the provision you need for a decent pension.

Table 20a: Monthly cost of a £60,000 pension mortgage

Borrower	Pension premium*	+ interest	= Total monthly payments	Term of loan (years)
Man aged 30	£122.57	+ £386.10	= £508.67	35
Man aged 40	£260.64	+ £386.10	= £646.74	25
Man aged 50	£652.74	+ £386.10	= £1,038.84	15

Net of basic rate tax relief at 25%. Includes life assurance cover for loan on death before retirement.

Table 20b: Projected results at retirement

Borrower	Total fund*	=	Annual pension**	+	Tax-free cash
Man aged 30	£268,000	=	£21,800	+	£67,000
Man aged 40	£258,000	=	£21,800	+	£64,600
Man aged 50	£250,000	=	£20,300	+	£62,500

This assumes that, in the event, investments will actually grow at 9% a year. However, the premiums have been calculated on the basis of an 8.5% growth rate, so there is some 'spare' tax-free cash after paying off the mortgage.
**This assumes an interest rate of 7.5% a year*

Source: Standard Life

Interest-only Mortgages

Finally, there are some lenders who are prepared to make interest-only mortgages available. In effect they are saying, 'We will lend you the money, and as long as you keep up with the interest on the loan, we don't care what means you use to pay back the capital, as long as you do it sometime.'

Again, there could be some circumstances where this facility might be useful – for example, to someone who is confident of receiving a large inheritance sometime in the future but is short of cash at present. All I would say is, don't imagine that spending a fiver on the lottery each week is adequate provision for paying back the capital!

6 ‖ *Choosing the Best Mortgage for You*

First-time buyers going into a building society for a mortgage today will, if that society is really on the ball, be offered a choice of three different types of mortgage: a repayment, an endowment, or a Pep. If they are lucky, they will get a brief explanation of the differences between these three repayment methods and, as they mutter, 'I'll have to think about it,' they will have three bits of paper pressed into their hands, showing the monthly cost of their loan with the three different options.

With nothing else to go on, borrowers study those three bits of paper and opt for the one with the lowest monthly cost. And that – depending on the assumptions used – could be any one of those three. Borrowers think they have made an informed choice, but in reality they have done little more than toss a coin up in the air to see which way it landed.

Twenty years ago four out of five borrowers took out repayment mortgages; the remainder chose endowments. That situation changed dramatically in the 1980s, with repayment mortgages the choice of just one in five and endowments being chosen by the rest. Since Pep mortgages became available only a few years ago they have been growing in popularity. By 1995 the positions were:

> **Endowments**: taken out by six in 10 borrowers
> **Repayments**: taken out by nearly three in 10
> **Pep and other types of mortgage**: taken out by around one in 10

So what has been responsible for this massive change, first one way, then the other? Part of the explanation lies in the fact that endowment and Pep mortgages are more lucrative for the lenders to sell. Building societies soon realized that they could generate massive profits from this source of business, so they started to emphasize the attractions of endowments.

But at the same time, during the 1980s the financial and economic conditions were such that it appeared to make a great deal of sense to choose an endowment over a repayment. Many of those conditions have now changed, and today the balance of economic factors is tilting back in favour of repayments.

It should be said right away that if you already have an endowment mortgage you should not necessarily think of abandoning it. There are other factors which may make it more sensible to stick with what you've got. But first-time buyers, with no existing arrangements, have complete freedom to choose.

Repayment Versus Endowment or Pep: the Basics

As the two previous chapters have detailed, the essential difference between these mortgages is this: with a repayment mortgage you pay back the capital as you go along. At the end of the chosen term, assuming you have kept up repayments in full, the entire loan will be paid off and that is the end of the matter.

With an endowment or Pep mortgage, you pay only interest on the loan, and at the same time start a separate savings plan which is invested mainly in shares. If the value of those investments grows as predicted at the outset, they produce exactly enough at the end of the term to pay off the loan. If they grow faster, you get a surplus; if they grow more slowly, either you will not have enough to pay off the loan – or, more likely, at some point along the way you will be asked to make extra monthly savings.

Repayment mortgages: advantages
Repayment mortgages score for a number of reasons. They are risk-free – in the sense that the capital is guaranteed to be paid back as long as you keep up with the mortgage payments. They can

be flexible: depending on your age, you can choose the length of the loan term, although 25 years is the term generally used for borrowers under 40.

If you move house later, you will have built up at least some equity in the property, so you will need to borrow less the next time. To be fair, this will not have much of an impact if you move after just a few years. In the early years of a mortgage, the amount of capital repaid grows very slowly, as Table 10 (see page 40) shows. Nevertheless, after only five years borrowers with repayment mortgages will have paid back nearly 8% of their capital, and this has important knock-on effects.

The most important relates to the mortgage indemnity guarantee. Borrowers taking out a loan of more than around 75% of the property's value are almost invariably hit with the extra cost of a mortgage indemnity guarantee, and the cost rises according to the percentage borrowed. The traditional system of charging is to ask borrowers for a small percentage of that part of the loan which exceeds 75%.

Chapter 7 (see page 40) goes into more detail but, as an example, the cost of an MIG with the Halifax on a property worth £100,000 is currently as follows:

Loan size	MIG rate	MIG premium
£80,000	4.15%	£207.50
£85,000	5.15%	£515.00
£90,000	6.15%	£922.50
£95,000	7.25%	£1,450.00

The more capital you can pay back, and the lower the percentage you have to borrow for the new property, the lower your MIG premium will be.

Repayments have other advantages as well. No one likes to think about it, but there could be times when you run into financial problems and find it hard to meet repayments. In such an emergency lenders will often allow borrowers to go temporarily onto an interest-only basis, cutting down the monthly cost immediately. And as the examples given in Tables 12 and 13 (see pages 47 and 49) show, you can juggle your repayment term to suit your changing life.

Repayment mortgages: drawbacks
There are no real drawbacks with a repayment mortgage. The only 'negative factors' are these:

- The repayment method does not in itself incorporate any life assurance, to cover the debt if you die before the end of the term. If you are making cost comparisons, remember to build in the extra cost of life cover before you start.
- The pace of capital repayment is extremely slow in the early years.
- And finally, at the end of the term, you have extinguished the debt, but – obviously – there is no extra surplus.

Endowment and Pep Mortgages

If things go well, endowment or Pep mortgages are the investment equivalent of a free lunch. You can get something for nothing, or at least quite a lot for a very little.

Looking first at the level of monthly payments, there is little to choose between the costs of a 25-year repayment mortgage plus life assurance, an endowment mortgage, and a Pep mortgage with added life cover. It's not easy to be categoric, because which one works out cheapest depends on the mortgage rate. At a low rate of interest – say 6% – the Pep is cheaper than the endowment by around £10 a month, which in turn is likely to be around £3 or £4 a month cheaper than the repayment option (these figures are for a £60,000 mortgage).

But this relationship changes as interest rates rise. Table 21 is a rough-and-ready indication of these differences. It assumes the borrower is a man aged 30 – we need this assumption in order to work out an appropriate life assurance premium. But you cannot take the precise figures as gospel, because different life companies charge different premiums and some are cheaper than others: your choice could make a difference of £5 or even £10 a month either way. In any case, if you don't fit into the category of 'man aged 30' the figures will be different.

Nevertheless, it's worth taking a quick look at the table, just to see how the relative positions of the three types of mortgage change with different interest rates. The broad message – that Peps and endowments get relatively more expensive as interest rates rise – remains true, whatever your age.

Table 21: The monthly costs of different mortgage methods on a loan of £60,000

Interest rate	Repayment	Endowment	Pep
6%	£380	£377	£367
7%	£415	£423	£413
8%	£450	£470	£460
9%	£488	£516	£506
10%	£525	£562	£552

Note: this table wraps up the basic mortgage cost for a 25-year £60,000 loan with an appropriate level of life assurance, using a decreasing term assurance policy for the repayment loan and a level term assurance policy for the Pep loan. The endowment has life assurance automatically built in. Premiums are based on single man aged 30.

Sources: Halifax, Standard Life, London & Country Mortgages

Something for (practically) nothing
So what do Peps and endowments offer? The answer is: the prospect of a lump sum surplus at the end of the term, which borrowers will get if the investment returns over the term of the loan exceed the growth rate assumed for setting the monthly savings level in the first place.

And here, as you may have guessed, we are approaching the $64,000 question. These days assumed rates of growth are generally set at 9% for a Pep (a tax-free investment) and 7 or 7.5%

for the endowment. At these levels, the price differential between repayments and these two forms of mortgage is small – of the order indicated in Table 21.

So then you must say to yourself, 'All right, I'm prepared to spend the extra £10 a month or whatever to get one of these mortgages. But what will I get in return for that?' And this is the real nub. If the investment returns from your chosen savings plan – endowment or Pep – turn out on average higher than the mortgage rate over the period of the loan, then you win. Not only will you get a cash surplus at the end of the loan, but you can be certain that that extra £10 a month or whatever you have been spending has produced a better return than you could have achieved by taking out the repayment mortgage and saving that extra sum on its own.

Mortgage rates versus investment returns: the future
Everything depends, therefore, on whether investment returns are likely to exceed the mortgage rate in the future. And this is where pure guess-work must take over from facts. In the past this has been the case – not always but usually. Table 22 shows the average annual growth rate from an equity investment compared to the average mortgage rate over various time periods.

Is it likely that the same pattern will repeat itself in the future? Frankly, it is impossible to answer that question if you are thinking about the next 25 years. But looking ahead on a much shorter time-span – say five years or so – there are two reasons to suggest the answer may be no.

The first is the cost of borrowing. This has risen in recent years in real terms – that is, after inflation has been taken into account. This is a world-wide phenomenon; in the UK we have had relatively high real interest rates for a good five years now, but this state of affairs shows no sign as yet of changing. And along with high rates we have also had cuts in the rate of tax relief available on mortgages. Until April 1991 the top rate of tax relief was 40% for high earners, and this applied to interest arising on the first £30,000 of the loan.

Table 22: Mortgage rates versus equity returns: long-term averages

Period	Mortgage rate (to end 1994)	Stockmarket returns	
		Annual average (gross)	Annual average (net)*
5 years	10.09%	9.8%	8.6%
10 years	11.57%	14.9%	13.6%
15 years	12.05%	18.6%	17.1%
20 years	11.78%	22.9%	21.2%
25 years	11.26%	15.5%	13.8%
50 years**	8.42%	13.1%	11.2%

These figures show the annual average return from the stockmarket, reinvesting the income either gross (which would be done in a Pep or pension fund) or net of basic rate tax. Note that these are notional figures based on a stockmarket index; 'real' investment would attract fund charges, which is likely to decrease the return by an average 1 to 1.5% a year.
**The stockmarket figures for the longest period are actually for 49 years only as this is the farthest they go back.*

Source: Chase de Vere Mortgage Management and BZW

Today the rate of relief is just 15% for everyone. Whether it will be reduced still further is getting into the realms of politics. However, it seems certain that the rate of tax relief will not be increased again, and is likely to be reduced still further – whichever political party is in power.

In the old days, whatever the actual mortgage rate, a top rate taxpayer was only paying 60% of that cost on at least the first £30,000 of his loan. That made it much more likely that investment returns, whatever they were, would exceed that rate. Today the situation is tougher.

And what of the outlook for investment returns? Once again, it must be anyone's guess over the longer term. In the short run, however, most experts believe that with our present low-inflation, investment returns are going to be relatively low compared with levels achieved in the recent past.

That is not to say it won't be worth investing in the stockmarket; but with an endowment or a Pep mortgage, you are in effect taking a gamble that investment returns from the stockmarket will exceed the cost of borrowing. It always was a gamble, though in past times it probably seemed like a near-certainty. Today the odds look different. Over 25 years, I would still guess the investment returns will come out on top; but I am by no means certain of that. I am only certain that the risk of their failing to do so now looks much bigger than it did.

Endowments and Pep mortgages: the drawbacks

We said at the start of this section that these two types of mortgage were the investment equivalent of a free lunch. And, as we all know, free lunches still have to be paid for by one means or another. You may think the investment risk described above is the biggest cost, but in fact there are a number of other potential drawbacks to choosing them. Some apply only to endowment mortgages, some to Peps as well.

Moving in the early years: with both Pep and endowment mortgages, borrowers are only paying interest on the loan and making no capital repayments. That means that when they move they still have the full amount outstanding. This, in turn, makes it more likely that their borrowing on a new property will be high in terms of the percentage borrowed against valuation, which usually means hefty MIG premium.

In any case, as we have already seen (see page 27), moving costs money – a good few thousand pounds whatever your circumstances – which endowment or Pep mortgage holders must find from their own resources. In the 'old' days, when property prices were rising quickly, this was not so much of a problem. You were practically guaranteed a profit every time you moved. Today you simply cannot rely on that. Property prices have been going nowhere for the last few years, as Figure 4 shows. This trend may change, but the latest report from the Halifax at the time of writing – inevitably, some months before publication – does not hold out any immediate hope for a change. It says: 'the underlying trend [of

Figure 4: House prices 1990–1995

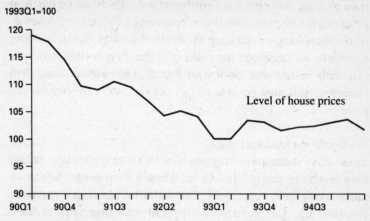

Source: Nationwide quarterly index

house prices] remains flat and we expect this situation to continue for the indefinite future.'

Lack of flexibility: repayment mortgages gradually build up a cushion of safety as borrowers make inroads into the total mortgage debt. They may be able to extend the term or go onto an interest-only basis if their income falls temporarily. With an endowment or Pep mortgage, there is no equivalent option.

Endowment policies are extremely inflexible schemes. Borrowers are committed to paying premiums at exactly the level imposed at the start. They usually cannot be increased, or reduced, or suspended – or at least, not without suffering some financial penalty. If you have a new-style mortgage endowment policy you may be required to increase premiums if, after a periodic review, it appears the original level of premiums will not grow to a sufficient sum to pay off the mortgage. But of course this is not the sort of flexibility that is likely to attract borrowers.

Cashing-in an endowment policy early also brings stiff penalties. For at least the first four to five years of the term you will be unlikely to get back even as much as you have paid in.

Peps are more flexible than endowments in this respect because their charges are imposed in a different way. There are no inherent penalties for stopping and, later, restarting a Pep savings scheme, or for increasing or reducing the level of savings. What is more, there are no penalties for cashing-in the Pep earlier than you originally anticipated. So if your Pep plan has grown faster than expected, you may be able to pay off the mortgage before you planned to.

Unravelling a joint mortgage

These days many joint mortgages need to be unravelled before they reach the end of their term. It could happen on divorce – a fairly likely occurrence with one in three marriages currently breaking up. Or perhaps two people who originally clubbed together to buy a home simply decide to go their separate ways.

Whatever the circumstances, if the mortgage was taken out on the basis of a joint endowment policy it instantly becomes awkward and messy to sort out. If both parties have contributed equally to the mortgage, you should by rights get half the endowment policy each. But you can only do that by cashing-in the policy, which is likely to be bad value for money.

There are ways round this problem. It could be avoided completely if couples took out two separate life policies at the outset; or the policy could be adapted to cover a single life only.

Pep mortgages are different: a plan can only be taken out by an individual, not jointly, so these problems do not arise.

Investments: Peps versus endowments

Investments in a life policy are taxed on both the income they produce and any capital gains realized. Pep investments are free of both taxes, so they should grow faster. Indeed, it is assumed that they will, which is why the level of monthly Pep savings required to pay off any given size of mortgage is lower than the premiums required under an endowment policy.

On the other hand, with-profits endowments are probably less risky investments than Peps, because life companies keep reserves to smooth out the peaks and troughs of investment returns.

So Which Mortgage Do I Choose?

I wish I could give simple, straightforward advice, but this is one of those questions where the more you know, the more you can appreciate the advantages and disadvantages on all sides.

Most of us have a number of different financial objectives in our lives, and most of us find it difficult to achieve all those objectives in the way we would like. We want, for instance:

- to buy our own homes and pay back the loan we have borrowed successfully
- to save cash in the short term for, say, holidays or home improvements, or to pay back various debts
- to save in the medium term for expenses like school or university fees
- to have some long-term savings for spending plans after retirement
- and, finally, to make sure we have a decent income after retirement to last out the rest of our lives.

Sorting out the various elements of financial planning by their different objectives is one way of categorizing them; most people will also accept that it is a sensible idea to separate out investments by their degree of risk, and to make sure they have a good spread of risk.

The appropriate degree of risk will to a large extent depend on your time horizon for that particular segment of your investments. For short-term savings it is sensible to keep your money in risk-free investments, like building society or bank deposit accounts. For medium-term investments you can take a bit more of a risk, and very long-term investments can involve much greater risk. All this is merely common sense.

But, in effect, a Pep or endowment mortgage is jumping in and muddying the waters – mixing up two quite different financial objectives which ought, by their nature, to be kept in quite separate patches of your risk spectrum. Supporters of Peps and endowments justify this by saying: 'Yes, a loan is something that has to be paid back and you shouldn't take too many risks with that. But the point about a mortgage is that it is very long term. And with such a long-term time horizon, it is all right to accept a greater degree of risk. And by doing this you can kill two birds with one stone. You can pay back your loan – *and* (with reasonable luck) build up some long-term savings for yourself.'

Only you can decide whether or not you feel happy with this line of reasoning. It is no use asking the experts for a definite answer on which mortgage will ultimately turn out to be the most profitable. Along with the rest of us, they *don't know*.

But while there's no certainty, there are, nevertheless, some useful pointers to which mortgage borrowers should choose. If you have read this far you will probably have more or less made up your own mind already, but just to summarize:

It is probably best to choose a repayment mortgage if any of the following statements apply to you:

- You expect to move within a few years, and are borrowing a high percentage of your property's value
- You are currently buying jointly but anticipate splitting up later on
- You have a fluctuating income
- Every penny counts
- You don't like taking risks – or perhaps you simply prefer to keep your long-term savings plans separate from your borrowings.

It might be sensible to take out an endowment or Pep mortgage if:

- You are prepared to take a calculated risk
- You are not expecting to move in the near future – or, if you are –

- You will not need to borrow a very high percentage of the property's value
- You welcome the prospect of being forced to make monthly savings, suspecting that otherwise you would never get around to it.

Finally, consider a pension mortgage if:

- You have the sort of job where you need to organize your own pension, and you realize that the only way you can persuade yourself to put in adequate amounts each month is to tie it up with your mortgage.

But if you do plump for the pension mortgage, make a mental note to review your decision in, say, five or 10 years' time. It could well be that the prospect of paying off the mortgage debt from your pension savings will look less and less appealing as time goes on, and you may decide later to convert it to a repayment mortgage instead.

What's irrevocable – and what isn't
The hardest decisions to take are those which have irrevocable consequences, so it is worth being clear about what you might be able to change if you later feel you've made a mistake – and what sort of costs this might involve.

Repayment mortgages: you are not committed to the term you choose at the outset. You can shorten or (sometimes) lengthen the term at any time, with no extra cost. You can pay back lump sums of capital at any time; and you can start up savings plans whenever you like. (Remember, however, if you've chosen a fixed or discounted rate mortgage, there could be redemption penalties for early repayment.)

Endowment mortgages: these are more inflexible. You can convert the loan to a repayment basis at any time, or pay off part of the capital with occasional lump sums, but what you cannot do is stop paying the regular endowment premiums or cash the policy in without incurring a financial penalty. As a rule of thumb, you should not expect to get back even the money you have paid in if you cash the policy in before it has been running for at least five years. And if you cash in even after 10 years of a 25-year policy, you could still get a rotten return for your money.

Pep mortgages: as with endowments, you can swap to a repayment loan and/or pay back capital. But the Pep plan itself is much more flexible: you can cash in at any time without penalty; you can increase Pep savings or reduce them, also without penalty.

The (Very) Last Word

Head reeling at this point? I must confess mine is. It is maddening to ask what seems to be a simple, straightforward question like: 'What sort of mortgage is best?' and to find that the answer goes on for pages, starting (and ending) with those dreadful words: 'it all depends . . .'

So here is my own personal answer in one paragraph (I cannot quite manage it in one sentence):

I think a repayment mortgage is probably best, partly because it is the obvious choice. There are some good arguments for taking out a Pep or an endowment mortgage, and if that is what you decide, I would not necessarily challenge your decision (indeed, I have one of these types of mortgage myself). But I would want you to work through the arguments first, appreciating the 'ifs and buts' of the endowment and Pep route, before you reach that decision.

Borrowers: the Awkward Bunch

If building societies could join a mortgage equivalent of Dateline, this is what they would be advertising for:

> NICE YOUNG borrower required, in an absolutely secure job with definite prospects of pay rises to come in the future. No big outgoings like alimony to pay, no record of past bad debts, and a good-sized cash pile to put down as a deposit. Evidence of behaviour as an exemplary borrower in the past especially welcome.

Many people are not going to fit into this neat category, and if you're one of them, don't despair: it is still perfectly possible to get a mortgage. The tricky thing is making sure you don't end up paying a great deal of money for it.

This chapter deals with the various categories of borrowers who, from the lender's point of view, are 'awkward', and provides hints on how you might save money.

You Want to Borrow a Lot

As we have seen, lenders charge borrowers extra if their loan is for (usually) 75% or more of the property's value. This cost usually takes the form of a one-off payment of a premium for a Mortgage Indemnity Guarantee. The MIG is an insurance policy, but the first thing to get clear is that although borrowers pay the premium, they get none of the benefit – that all belongs to the lender: if the borrower defaults on the loan and the lender repossesses the house and sells it to recoup its debt, then any shortfall between the sale price and the original loan is made up by the insurance.

A decade ago, with house prices rising steeply each year, this sort of policy was money for old rope as far as the insurance company was concerned. As long as the borrower had lived in his house for a year or so, the resale price was almost certain to be higher than the original price paid, so the risk of a shortfall was extremely remote – although that did not stop fairly hefty premiums being charged. But today, with house prices static, the risk is appreciably greater, and the MIG premiums even more hefty. (Incidentally, these days lenders use all sorts of different names for the MIG, such as a 'fee for additional mortgage security' or 'scheme for maximum advances'. In effect it's all the same thing.)

There are basically two systems used by lenders to work out the MIG charge for someone borrowing a high percentage loan: one is based on the formula used by the Halifax, the other on the Nationwide's method, but as you can see from Tables 23 and 24, the end result is much the same.

With the Halifax system, borrowers pay a premium according to the amount borrowed in excess of 75%. The premium *rate* depends on how high a percentage is borrowed and rises in tiers. The premium *amount* depends on the applicable rate and the size of your loan. The premium rate is applied only to that portion of borrowing which exceeds the 75% level.

With Nationwide, borrowers pay a higher mortgage rate on their entire loan for the first year if they are borrowing more than 75%. This interest rate surcharge also rises in tiers. Note that, at the time of writing, Nationwide will consider lending 100% of a property's value, whereas the Halifax will only lend up to a maximum of 95%.

As you can see from the tables, it is not a disaster if you have to borrow a little bit in excess of 75% of the property value. You may not like paying an extra £150 or £200, but in the context of an £80,000 loan it is not an enormous amount. But the expense rises rapidly the higher you clinb up that percentage ladder, and it is worth exploring ways in which to avoid or cut that charge.

Let us take an easy case to begin with: you have found a

Table 23: The cost of mortgage indemnity guarantees

(a) **The Halifax system**

Loan as % of property value	*Premium per every £100 extra borrowed in excess of 75%*
up to 75%	none
over 75% up to 80%	4.15%
over 80% up to 85%	5.15%
over 85% up to 90%	6.15%
over 90% up to 95%	7.25%

(b) **The Nationwide system**

Loan as % of property value	*Additional interest on entire loan for first year*
up to 75%	nil
over 75% up to 80%	0.2%
over 80% up to 85%	0.6%
over 85% up to 90%	1.2%
over 90% up to 95%	1.6%
over 95% up to 100%	3.0%

Table 24: Examples of the cost of MIGs in practice

Property worth £100

Loan size	*Mortgage indemnity cost*	
	Halifax	*Nationwide*
£75,000	nil	nil
£80,000	£207,50	£151.00
£85,000	£515.00	£483.00
£90,000	£922.50	£1,026.00
£95,000	£1,450.00	£1,448.00
£100,000	n.a.	£2,865.00

Source: Halifax, Nationwide Building Societies

property valued at £70,000, and you have exactly £10,000 saved as a deposit. The Halifax (let us suppose) offers you a mortgage, and tells you its 'Additional Mortgage Security Fee' (in other words, the MIG) works out at £461.25.

At this point you should get out your calculator. You want to borrow £60,000 on a £70,000 property, which works out at 85.7% – just above one of the tiers on the Halifax charging structure. If you can find another £500 to put down as a deposit, your loan will be for £59,500, or exactly 85% of the value, which brings you down a tier.

Borrow £60,000, and the additional fee works out at 6.15% of the excess borrowed over 75% (or £52,500) of the loan – in other words, 6.15% of £7,500. Borrow £59,500, and the additional fee is 5.15% of £7,000. The result of these two sums? A £60,000 loan has an additional fee of £461.25; a £59,500 loan, an additional fee of £360.50.

The moral is clear – it is always worth checking to see exactly where you are within the tiered structure of charges; it may well pay you to find that bit extra to put down as a deposit. And if you don't have it, borrow it – preferably from some source such as parents, who might countenance making an interest-free loan to their nearest and dearest. If you are not lucky enough to have parents like that, it could even be worth borrowing it on your credit card. Taking out a one-year loan for £500 on your credit card will cost around £58 in interest, compared to the £100-plus saving on the additional fee.

Table 25 gives one more example to help you get the picture, once again using the Halifax system.

Plan (b) represents a saving of £237.50 over plan (a). And don't forget, of course, that if you are able to find that extra £1,000, there will also be immediate savings on interest costs on the mortgage itself – a matter of £80-odd per year.

If you cannot find the extra cash yourself, or do not wish to borrow it, it is still worth trying to cut down the fee by renegotiating a lower price with the sellers. Try asking them for a reduction in the price so that your loan will fall a tier; if that fails, ask if they will meet the cost of the fee itself. No holds are barred in this negotiating game, and sometimes sellers will respond positively to a request for a reduction of, say, £461 to meet the extra fee,

Table 25: Purchase of house valued at £100,000

(a)	**Borrower has £9,000 deposit**	
	Loan amount	£91,000
	Additional security fee rate	7.25% on £16,000 (£91,000 − £75,000)
	Additional security fee cost	**£1,160**
(b)	**Borrower has £10,000 deposit**	
	Loan amount	£90,000
	Additional security fee rate	6.15% on £15,000 (£90,000 − £75,000)
	Additional security fee cost	**£922.50**

whereas if you ask for a £1,000 drop in the price previously agreed you may just get a blanket refusal.

Finally, you should note that some lenders let you add the cost of this fee onto the loan, which will then be repaid over the whole of the mortgage term; others let you pay in instalments over 12 months (in effect, this is what the Nationwide system requires you do to); but in certain cases borrowers may have to pay the fee in cash. This is especially likely where loan percentages are very high – 95% or above.

Split loans
Another way of reducing the cost on a high percentage loan is to go for a 'split' loan. You will probably need a good mortgage broker to arrange this, though in theory you might be able to organize something similar yourself.

For example, one packaged product on the market as I write splits the loan, with 90% being lent by a big building society and the remaining 10% by a bank. This has three advantages: firstly, borrowers pay an MIG fee to the building society at the 90% rate, rather than the higher rates charged on higher percentage borrowing. Secondly, borrowers can get a decent fixed or discounted rate for this portion of the loan. Many of the societies' 'special offers' for new mortgages only apply to loans not exceeding 90% of the purchase price, so this second advantage can be a valuable one. Finally, borrowers will be able to add the cost of the MIG fee to their loan, which is not usually possible if they are borrowing the full 100% from a single borrower.

Inevitably there is a downside to this type of arrangement. The interest rate charged on the top 10% of the loan is usually considerably higher than the normal mortgage rate. Roughly speaking, if the mortgage rate is around 8.5%, the top-up rate is likely to be around 11.5%.

If you crunch all the numbers, however – which mortgage brokers will do routinely – the total cost of the package will still work out cheaper than going for 100% loan from a single lender.

Beware of the fakes

Not all 100% mortgages are what they seem. One big lender which claims to offer 100% loans requires borrowers to pay an MIG premium of 10% on the amount borrowed above 70% of the property value; this premium cannot be added to the loan, so it must be paid in cash. If you are buying a house valued at £100,000, for example, you must still find £2,500 in cash (10% of £25,000); but the reason you need the 100% loan in the first place is because you have not got any cash!

You Don't Have a Steady Job

Whether you are self-employed or an employee working on a short-term contract, you are, in theory, a less attractive borrower to the main mortgage lenders than people who have 'proper' full-time jobs. That does not mean you will be unable to get a loan; but you may well have to pay more for it. There are special loan schemes available for people who find it hard to produce proof of their income, known as 'non-status mortgages' or 'self-certification mortgages', but I advise you to avoid these if possible – they tend to be more expensive than the ordinary loans.

Despite the apparent evidence to the contrary, there are no hard and fast rules here. In theory, to qualify for a mainstream loan from a mortgage lender, the self-employed must provide audited accounts for the last three years as proof of their income. This has two immediate drawbacks for such borrowers: many may not have been self-employed for the requisite length of time; moreover, the taxable profit shown by many self-employed individuals may be less than a corresponding employee's salary, thus cutting down their potential ability to borrow. This is not, I hasten to add, because the self-employed are tax cheats, but because they are taxed under a different system. Self-employed people can, quite legitimately, put more of their daily expenses against tax, but to the untutored eye of a building society clerk, it may look as if they are simply poorer.

The best way to approach the problem is to realize that you have a selling job on your hands. Remember that building societies and banks are managed and staffed by employees, and employees do not always understand or appreciate what life is like on the other side of the fence. They all, ostensibly, have rules on how they will treat the self-employed and, while those rules may be broken, you cannot expect the counter-clerk at your local society to break them for you.

You will need to go to managerial level, and it would be an excellent idea to enlist the help of your accountant. You should point out the positive advantages of being self-employed: unlike an employee, you cannot be sacked; and while your income is likely to fluctuate, it is unlikely to disappear altogether unless all your customers or clients simultaneously take it into their heads to dispense with your services or refuse to buy your goods. And then you could point out that running your own business means you have to be financially responsible – you are much less likely than some feckless employees to get yourself into a tangle with unpaid credit card bills, for example.

My feeling is that the big mortgage lenders have yet to come to terms with the current changes in working patterns. If it is true that straightforward full-time, long-term employment is on the decline and short-term contracts and self-employment on the increase, then one of these days lenders will have to work out how to lend to such people; otherwise they will have fewer and fewer customers.

As a self-employed person asking for a loan, you should view your task as an educational one; moreover, you'll be paving the way for all those other self-employed people who will be coming along later!

And finally, recognize the realities of the situation: if you're going to get a black mark as a borrower for being self-employed, make sure you score some brownie points as well. For example, have a decent-sized deposit to put down; come up with concrete evidence of a good long-term record as a saver or as a repayer of debts.

You Have a Bad Credit Record

All lenders operate a form of credit scoring before they decide whether to lend anyone money. 'Credit scoring' sounds scientific, but it is a matter of judgement as much as fact. In effect what happens is this: lenders gather all sorts of relevant information about you as a prospective borrower – your employment history, your past record of paying back debts, how you handle your credit card borrowing and whether you are an existing customer (either as a saver or a borrower).

All these different bits of information are awarded points, and once the total is totted up it will indicate what sort of borrower you are likely to be. Abbey National, for example, has four basic categories: 'low risk', 'normal', 'proceed with caution' and 're-commend refusal'.

At least some of the information used comes from credit reference agencies. There are two major agencies operating in the UK, Equifax Europe and CCN, which all mortgage lenders are likely to use. They collect a range of financial data on individuals, including whether they have any county court judgements recorded against them for bad debts, and details of how they have run any financial accounts over the last six years. If you get turned down for a loan, the lender is unlikely to tell you exactly why, but it should tell you if one of the factors was the information from a credit reference agency. It should also tell you which credit reference agency was used.

If you want to take the matter further, you can find out precisely what information the agency holds on you: individuals have a statutory right to see this on payment of a fee of £1. Suppose some of this information is incorrect? Then you have a further statutory right to require the agency to amend its files within 28 days of receiving your request.

And then, if you do not think an amendment is satisfactory, you can ask for an explanatory note, written by you, to be included in your file. At this stage the agency can still refuse to include the note if it thinks it is 'defamatory, incorrect, frivolous or scandalous' and can ask the Director General of Fair Trading to make a ruling.

This is all very well if the information held is indeed incorrect – but what if it is all too true? There is no need for instant despair if one lender turns you down, because they all have different lending criteria and one may accept where another declines.

Nevertheless, it may be as well to enlist the help of a good mortgage broker who will have close relationships with a number of lenders and be able to argue your case with them – and at the right level within the organization. It may not always work – some cases may just be too hopeless – but it is definitely worth persisting.

Finally, there's another large group of mortgage borrowers who pose problems from a lender's point of view: the 'negative equity' sufferers – those who bought a property some years ago when property prices were higher than they are now, and are stranded with a mortgage bigger than the value of their home. Their problems – and the possible solutions – are dealt with in the next chapter.

8 ‖ *Second-Time Buyers*

Second-time buyers might be forgiven for thinking that first-time buyers have all the fun. They don't have to sell a property before they can buy one; they are not lumbered with any negative equity; and, as often as not, the cream of the mortgage offers are sternly labelled 'first-time buyers only'. What's more, first-time buyers can – if they are bright enough – benefit from the horrible experiences of others who have suffered in the property market during the last few years, without having to pay for it themselves. In sum, it is an unfair world.

It is tempting to think that absolutely everyone who now qualifies as a 'second-time buyer' is afflicted with negative equity – having a mortgage greater than the current resale value of their property. The figures are enormous – in mid-1995 over a million homebuyers were thought to be in this situation. Nevertheless, it does not apply to everyone, and in the first section of this chapter I will look at the best mortgage gambits for the relatively problem-free second-timers – those without negative equity.

Mortgages For the Second Time Around

Choosing a mortgage for a second purchase is an excellent time to take stock of your overall financial position. This second purchase could well be your last – or at any rate, the last before retirement and a country cottage beckons. So it is worth pushing up the periscope and trying to take a long-distance view of your career and overall financial aims.

By 'early middle' age many people have a clear idea of how their career is progressing, and whether, indeed, they want to stay on a conventional career path or to branch off into a more independent and interesting existence in the years to come. Choosing the right mortgage at this stage could be a vital part of any plans to become more independent.

The odds are, if you first bought a property some five or 10 years ago, that your existing mortgage is an endowment one. The obvious course of action is to continue with that choice, but you don't have to. It would not be wise to stop paying premiums into the policy, or to cash it in, because both courses of action are basically bad value for money. But you can keep the policy running, and still have a repayment mortgage on your new property; or, perhaps, a split mortgage, with the original proportion on an interest-only basis, backed by your endowment policy, and the remainder on a repayment basis. Or you could take out a Pep mortgage for the remainder.

In fact the permutations are almost endless, and it is up to you to decide. Table 26 details the options open to a couple who are moving house after 10 years. This is simply to give you an idea of what the decision-making process involves; don't feel you have to follow, or grasp, every single detail. As so often in matters like these, it will all fall into place once you are considering your own circumstances.

Table 26: The mortgage choice for second-time buyers

Tom and Harriet have a £60,000 endowment mortgage on a property bought 10 years ago. They are trying to decide what type of mortgage to take out on their new property for which they need an £80,000 loan. The capital outstanding on the existing mortgage is £60,000; the endowment policy matures in 15 years' time.

They jot down what they see as the main options, together with their costs, and then consider the overall pluses and minuses of the various alternatives. The one thing they are certain about is that they want to keep the existing endowment policy running until maturity to avoid any early surrender penalties. But then the hard choices start.

Ideally, they want to keep their repayment within the original time-frame, so the whole lot is repaid 15 years from now. But they are not sure whether they will be able to afford this, so they divide their options initially into two sections: the first four detailing their choices for a complete repayment within 15 years, the second four allowing for the extra £20,000 to be repaid over a longer period.

First choice: Full repayment in 15 years

OPTION 1

Keep the original endowment policy unaltered, and take out an additional policy for £20,000 over 15 years so that the whole mortgage is repaid at once.

	Monthly cost
Existing endowment premium	£80.00
Extra endowment premium, 15-year term	£75.00
Mortgage interest on full £80,000	£535.00
Total	**£690.00**

OPTION 2

Keep the endowment policy running to pay off the first £60,000 after 15 years, and then put remaining £20,000 on a repayment basis, also over 15 years. Need life assurance for the extra £20,000 in the form of a Mortgage Protection Policy.

	Monthly cost
Existing endowment premium	£80.00
15-year repayment mortgage top-up	£201.00
Life cover top-up	£9.00
Mortgage interest on £60,000	£393.00
Total	**£683.00**

OPTION 3

Keep the endowment policy running, but purely as a savings policy, and put the whole £80,000 new loan onto a repayment basis over 15 years. Life cover, in the form of a Mortgage Protection Policy, is only required for the £20,000 extra – the existing endowment will protect the rest.

	Monthly cost
Existing endowment premium	£80.00
15-year £80,000 repayment mortgage	£788.50
Life cover top-up on £20,000	£9.00
Total	**£877.50**

OPTION 4

Keep the endowment policy running, and 'top up' with a Pep mortgage, also lasting for 15 years. Here, a level term assurance policy to cover the extra £20,000 is required.

	Monthly cost
Existing endowment premium	£80.00
Pep premium over 15 years	£61.00
Level term life cover top-up	£11.00
Mortgage interest on £80,000	£535.00
Total	**£687.00**

Second choice: Repayment of £60,000 over 15 years, with the remaining £20,000 repaid over 25 years

OPTION 5

As (1) but make the top-up endowment policy for a 25-year term.

	Monthly cost
Existing endowment premium	£80.00
Extra endowment premium	£38.00
Mortgage interest on full £80,000	£535.00
Total	**£653.00**

OPTION 6

As (2) but arrange the £20,000 repayment mortgage over 25 years. Need a Mortgage Protection Policy.

	Monthly cost
Existing endowment premium	£80.00
25-year repayment mortgage top-up	£163.00
Life cover top-up	£11.00
Mortgage interest on £60,000	£393.00
Total	**£647.00**

OPTION 7

As (3) but arrange the repayment over 25 years. Here, need to take out a Mortgage Protection Policy for the full £80,000,

	Monthly cost
Existing endowment premium	£80.00
25-year £80,000 repayment mortgage	£636.00
Life cover on £80,000	£37.00
Total	**£753.00**

OPTION 8

As (4) but organize the Pep top-up so it should repay the extra £20,000 after 25 years. Level term assurance needed.

	Monthly cost
Existing endowment premium	£80.00
Pep premium over 25 years	£23.00
Level term life cover top-up	£14.50
Mortgage interest on £80,000	£535.00
Total	**£652.50**

Two of these options – 3 and 7 – stick out like sore thumbs: they are much more expensive than the rest. This is scarcely surprising because both involve freeing up the existing endowment policy completely. Nice as it might be to have £60,000-odd coming to them in 15 years' time without the need to pay the mortgage off with it, Tom and Harriet decide that those two options are simply too expensive.

However, the encouraging thing they have learned from this exercise is that it is not very much more expensive to repay the whole loan within their original time frame, and that is the first decision they take. Their choices have now been narrowed down to options 1, 2 and 4 – the monthly cost differs by only a few pounds.

So which is it to be? Being real, perverse human beings rather than perfect examples, they decide on option 4, using a Pep as the vehicle for the top-up mortgage – only they decide they can actually save £75 a month into the Pep rather than the £61 demanded. They reckon that will provide them with a useful safety net if the Pep investments do not grow as quickly as expected (9% a year) – and if the Pep does perform well, they will be able (if they wish) to pay off the £20,000 part of their loan before the end of the 15-year term and save a useful bit of mortgage interest. On the other hand, Harriet's Tax Exempt Special Savings Account is coming up for maturity in a couple of years' time, and they might use *that* to pay off some of the loan.

Obviously, 'Tom and Harriet' is only one possible scenario among many, and there is no single 'right' answer to the question of what sort of mortgage to get second time around. It depends on where you're coming from, as well as where you see yourself going. But the following three points may be worth bearing in mind.

Repayment mortgages
If your original mortgage was a repayment one, you may well be inclined to choose the same vehicle this time round. If so, the temptation may be to start a fresh 25-year term with the new loan. But do you really want to extend your mortgage-paying days yet further? Look at Table 15 (page 52) to see how the figures work out.

If you are trading up and borrowing a great deal more than previously, you may be especially inclined to opt for the longest available term in order to cut costs. But you might be able to compromise. For instance, if you are 10 years into your current 25-year repayment mortgage, you might be able to afford the new loan on a 20-year basis, even if you cannot manage the payments required for a 15-year loan.

Pension mortgages
If your first loan was a pension mortgage, you should take careful stock of your overall financial planning before deciding what to do next time. At 30, pensions seem almost as remote as the chances of winning the lottery, and a great deal more boring; by 40, they start getting rather more interesting; and by the age of 50, pensions become practically the most important part of anyone's financial life.

Should you be increasing your pension savings? Would you like to take early retirement – or start a venture of your own with a retirement income to back you up?

Before deciding whether to continue on the pension mortgage route, you'll need answers to all these questions. For many people it will probably be a good idea to free up their pension fund from the burden of having to repay the mortgage debt, when they get the opportunity to do so.

That is not to say it is always a bad idea to take out a pension mortgage in the first place. It can be a useful way of persuading young people to make at least some start on saving for their pension, at an age when they might not feel particularly inclined to do so. But it is important to reassess that decision as you get older.

Endowment mortgages

Should you cash in your endowment policy when you move? The basic rule of thumb is 'never cash in a policy early' – it is simply bad value. But under certain circumstances it might be worthwhile. If you are having to borrow a high percentage of your new property's value, the cost of the mortgage indemnity guarantee can be very high. Cashing-in the existing endowment could allow you to escape this MIG cost; and, further, it might allow you to qualify for a favourable mortgage deal.

Many of the mortgage 'best buys' are only open to borrowers who can put down 10% or more of the purchase price. A good mortgage broker should be able to work out figures to give you a reasonable basis on which to judge.

Negative Equity

'Negative equity' is a phrase coined in the early 1990s to describe the situation – hitherto unprecedented – of borrowers who owed more on their mortgage than their home was worth. It is not necessarily a problem – either to lenders, as long as the loan repayments are kept up to date, or to borrowers, as long as they do not want to move house.

But many of those in negative equity *do* want to move, and because their mortgage loan is secured on the house, the only way they can normally change properties is by coming up with cash for the difference between the price their house fetches and the value of their loan.

It is not impossible to move house if you are stuck in negative equity; but it may be tough. The only really useful advice to give in this situation is of no use if you need to move now: and that is to pay back as much capital as possible, *before* you get to this point. If you are still reading this section, you obviously have not done so or, at any rate, not enough to get yourself completely out of this debt trap. Given the way property prices have plummeted in past years, especially in the hardest-hit regions like London and East Anglia, I can only say you have all my sympathy.

The first place to start is to work out who, if anyone, you can tap for a 'soft loan'. If you need to move because of work, try your employer. If your parents have plenty of money, ask if they would be prepared to make a loan; it does not have to be a case of sponging, you could offer them the going rate of interest on a building society savings account. For them, it may mean no financial loss, but for you it represents considerable financial gain.

If you have an endowment mortgage, it may be worth getting an estimate of the surrender value of your policy and seeing whether this would solve your problem of negative equity. This goes against the grain of financial sense – surrendering policies early is almost always bad value for money – but it may be the best option in these circumstances.

A better alternative may be to *sell* the policy to someone else on the 'second-hand' endowment market. In many cases sellers can get significantly better prices by selling than by surrendering the policy back to the life company. The drawback is that most of the market makers in this field prefer policies that have been running for a good period of time – say, 10 years out of an original term of 25. A few, however, will consider policies that have been running for just six or seven years.

The price obtained depends on the particular company your policy is with – some companies attract better prices than others – and it must be a 'with-profits' policy rather than a unit-linked one. But it is definitely worth trying; one company of market makers, for example, has recently bought endowment policies that had been running for six or seven years for between 24% and 35% above their respective surrender values. The Association of Policy Marketmakers (see Appendix, page 133) will put you in touch with firms that specialize in this market.

For many people, though, none of these options will be available. In that case your best port of call is your current mortgage lender. And this is where luck comes in: if your original mortgage was with a lender such as the Halifax, Nationwide, Woolwich or one of a number of other building societies or banks, you should at least get a ready hearing, and I believe the situation is gradually improving. A couple of years ago scarcely any lender was prepared to make negative equity loans; now many will do so, and as they gain experience of lending on these terms they realize that the world will not come to an end and they are more willing to repeat the process.

The three lenders mentioned above – and others – have all launched formal schemes to help people with negative equity to move house. The Woolwich, for example, has three different schemes. Its 'Parentline' allows borrowers to transfer the negative equity on to their parents' homes (assuming the latter are willing!); the 'mobility mortgage' allows borrowers to move house and take the negative equity with them (under this scheme borrowers cannot take out a larger loan than they have already); finally, it offers a 'negative equity mortgage', which allows those borrowers who can prove they can afford it to take out a large loan on moving – up to 125% of the value of their new property, with the provision that the unsecured portion must be no more than £25,000. The Halifax operates a similar scheme to this last one but stipulates that the unsecured portion must be on a repayment basis with a maximum loan term of 20 years.

With these two lenders, borrowers can qualify for any of the society's fixed or discounted rates, though with other lenders you may find you are obliged to borrow at their full basic rate. Nevertheless, at around 8.4% (at the time of writing), this is still a bargain compared with unsecured loan rates of 15 to 20%-plus. In any case, unsecured personal loans are generally only set up for a maximum term of five years (very occasionally 10) but either way, the monthly payments are vastly more expensive than an ordinary mortgage.

The lenders who operate these special schemes will only consider you if you are an existing borrower with them; if you are not currently with one of these, you will have to try to persuade your current lender to do something for you.

Table 27 provides a summary of what some of the major mortgage lenders were willing to do for their 'negative equity' borrowers in the summer of 1995. While these terms will not necessarily still be on offer when you read this, I don't believe that lenders will make them less favourable and it is even possible they may improve as lenders gain confidence in this field.

Table 27: Negative equity schemes

Lender	Deposit required	Maximum percentage lending	Maximum negative equity	Maximum repayment term (years)
Halifax	No	125%	£25,000	20
Abbey National	5%	125%	£25,000	25
Nationwide	No	125%	£25,000	25
Woolwich	5%	125%	£25,000	20
Alliance & Leicester	No	125%	£25,000	10
Britannia	5%	125%	£25,000	10
National & Provincial	No	–	£25,000	10
Bristol & West	No	125%	£25,000	10–15
Yorkshire	5%	depends on circumstances		25
Bradford & Bingley	No	— depends on circumstances —		
Barclays	5%	125%	depends	10
Lloyds	No	130%	£30,000	15

Note: In this table the maximum percentage lending relates to the maximum lent on the new property's value, and the maximum term relates to the speed at which the negative equity portion must be repaid. In most cases, the interest rate for the whole loan is at the lender's usually basic rate, but Bristol & West charged a 1% loading on the negative equity portion.

If your mortgage is not with one of these, the table may serve as a useful crib sheet – or encouragement – to persuade your own lender to come up with a similar scheme. It may be a good idea to enlist the help of a good mortgage broker in this situation, though I have known cases of people who have succeeded in persuading their lenders on their own.

So how do you go about it? What you must do is persuade them that you are an excellent credit risk. Point out to them how you have kept up repayments throughout the period of high interest rates; provide proof of your income and show them how this has risen since you first took out your mortgage, and how much lower a proportion of your monthly income the mortgage payments consitute these days.

Present a well-argued case as to why you need to move now – family or work reasons – and suggest, perhaps, that the unsecured portion of the loan (the 'negative equity' part) be put on a faster payment schedule – 15 years rather than 25, say – than the balance. Point out to them what other lenders are prepared to offer – and suggest that if the Halifax, the Woolwich and all these others can help their customers, your lender should be able to do so too.

It is impossible to be categoric, of course, but this strategy has been known to work. One key factor to your success is getting through to the right level in the organization. Clerks are not paid to break or bend the rules; you will have to fight your way up to manager level.

All this assumes, naturally, that you have kept right up to date with your repayments, that you are still in a job and that your income has risen since you took out the loan. If none of this is true, then I would not want to hold out false hopes – I suspect your chances of getting a mortgage to cover the negative equity on a move are just about zero. Keep buying those lottery tickets if you must, but if you do want to move sometime in the future there is only one way out: put every spare penny you have into paying back extra on the mortgage.

But what about property prices: won't they, at least eventually, move upwards and cancel out the negative equity? In the long run, no doubt, but as the economist John Maynard Keynes pointed out, in the long run we are all dead, and I suspect most people who want to move out of their current homes are not planning to wait until they do so feet first.

Negative equity: cases that don't fit the schemes
However good a borrower you are, help may be denied you if your circumstances do not fit. Although the schemes outlined above can effectively beat the problem of negative equity in straightforward cases, a problem remains where homebuyers currently have two properties. I suspect there are many cases of couples who have been 'stranded' with a surplus flat or house from their single days which is impossible to sell because they cannot make up in cash the difference between the sale price and the loan. The mortgage is probably not with the same lender as the mortgage on the property they now occupy, so their position is not good: lender A, the one with the 'spare' property and the negative equity, has no motive for helping because the main mortgage is elsewhere; lender B is equally unwilling to take in lender A's dirty washing – as long as its mortgage is being repaid properly, why should it worry?

This seems short-sighted to me: lender B's position would actually be more secure if the couple were not struggling to meet two sets of mortgage interest. But officially, at least, practically no lender has a scheme that can help in these circumstances – and lenders do like 'schemes'. The Woolwich Building Society is the sole exception to this general rule, as far as I have been able to find out; it will consider helping out its existing borrowers whether it is in the position of lender A or lender B. All the others questioned on this topic simply said 'no'.

On the other hand, I do know of a particular case where a lender was persuaded to act. In this case the couple concerned ('John and Mary') had two mortgages totalling £84,000 – a £40,000 loan on a studio flat John had bought some years earlier, which had since fallen in value to £27,000, and a £44,000 loan on Mary's house, where they were now living, which was worth £46,000. In this case lender B (with the mortgage on the house) simply did not want to know. But lender A listened – after some persuasion. At first, it wanted to get the couple to sell the house and move back into the flat. Then it accepted this was unreasonable. After more negotiation it agreed to allow the flat sale to go through, and transfer the negative equity – £13,000 – onto the couple's house, as a second charge on the property. The end result was that the couple cut their mortgage from £84,000 to £57,000 and were able to continue living in their house. As for the lenders, in my view both should have been happy with the change; their loans were much more secure now that the couple were not having to meet massive mortgage bills each month.

Homebuyers with a real problem on their hands are those who bought 'first-time buyers' properties in the mid- to late-1980s. Today's first-time buyers are shunning such properties, and rightly so. In the current economic climate these types of property are only really suitable for renting.

Letting your property
Many borrowers with negative equity and a 'surplus' property have already become reluctant landlords, renting out the flat they cannot sell. Couples who have started living together in the last few years may have had no option if both partners have bought their own properties; while they have no need of the two homes, they cannot afford to sell. If borrowers are lucky, the rent may cover the mortgage interest, but there is not likely to be any sort of profit; indeed a shortfall is more common.

I suspect that most people in this situation have not divulged the let to their mortgage lender, although the terms of the mortgage usually oblige them to do so. Lenders are apt to charge extra on the mortgage rate – typically 0.25% or more – where property is rented out, so this omission is understandable, to say the least.

Nevertheless, it is worth bearing two points in mind. Firstly, you should definitely inform your insurance company if you have tenants; if you do not, and subsequently have to make a claim, the insurance company could well refuse to pay it. Secondly, so long as you keep up with your mortgage payments, keeping your lender in the dark may not pose an immediate problem; but suppose you fall into arrears? At this point, if it starts repossession proceedings, the lender will find out, and you may have forefeited any right to be treated generously.

Finally, if you do intend to rent out property, it is well worth doing it properly – with a legal agreement on a shorthold tenancy basis – to protect your security as landlord. A lender may be able to advise you on the best way to proceed.

Government help for negative equity sufferers?

Back-bench Tory MPs have periodically been clamouring for government help to be given to those who suffer negative equity. So far, the government has refused to listen, but you can be sure that if it does, it will be headline news so sufferers will not be left in ignorance. However, I have to say that I don't think it likely that any help will be forthcoming. Certainly it would be unwise to count on it.

‖ *How to Buy Freeholds,*
Houseboats, or Country Cottages

Flat-owners

The Leasehold Reform, Housing and Urban Development Act 1993 gave important new rights to flat-owners in England and Wales. They can collectively buy the freehold of their block, or individually purchase an extension of their lease.

Nearly all owner-occupied flats in England and Wales were originally 'leasehold', which means their owners purchased a long-term lease (typically 99 years, though occasionally one sees leases for 999 years). At the end of the term, the property reverts to the freeholder, who has in the interim been paid a fairly nominal annual ground rent on the property. The leaseholder has nothing at the end of the term.

With very long leases, this distinction between freehold and leasehold is of little more than academic interest. But the problems of a declining lease can start to make themselves felt surprisingly early.

Most mainstream mortgage lenders will only consider lending on normal terms if the lease has at least 25 years to run after completion of the mortgage term. This means that a lease of 50 years can only just squeeze into the definition of 'normal' if the borrower wants an ordinary 25-year mortgage. And there would be no hope of selling to anyone else on such terms, which means that leases of 60 years or even 70 years are beginning to look like a bad deal.

This legislation is therefore extremely important for lease-holders, and either route offered – buying the freehold or extending the lease – could be a good solution to their problems. There are a number of legal hoops to be negotiated in each case – firstly, to ascertain if you are eligible under the Act, and secondly, to complete the process. This section can only give a very basic outline of what is a fairly complex piece of legislation; if you are interested in going ahead you will need expert legal help and advice.

Buying the freehold

This must be a collective effort from you and at least two-thirds of all other 'qualifying tenants' in the block of flats. Qualifying tenants are, broadly, those holding leases with an original term of at least 21 years, who pay a nominal or low ground rent, and whose property is not excluded by other provisions in the Act (for example, if the freehold is owned by a charitable housing trust or is situated within a cathedral boundary). There are numerous other provisos, but, on the whole, most people with 'normal' flats, either purpose-built in a block, or conversions within a large house, are likely to qualify.

The cost of the freehold will depend on a whole raft of circumstances, but the Act lays down some quite specific principles on how it should be calculated: the freeholder is entitled to at least half the 'marriage value' from selling the freehold. 'Marriage value' can broadly be defined as the additional value which is created when leasehold and freehold interests are brought together; but in practice, the amount asked, and eventually paid, depends on the negotiating strengths of the parties involved.

Where flats have very long leases, the freehold value may be little more than the capital value of the ground rents: as a minimum, you would expect to pay between seven and 10 times the annual ground rent. But 'marriage value' might add considerably to this. The Act also stipulates that buyers must pay any (reasonable) legal and other costs incurred by the freeholder in selling.

In practice, the biggest obstacle to buying the freehold, apart from negotiating a reasonable price, may be getting other lease-holders to agree to join in. But the benefits go beyond protecting the capital value of your property and escaping the problems of a declining lease. There is an immediate saving in ground rent, and as you will be managing the property yourself you will no longer have expensive (and possibly inefficient) managing agents to pay. None the less, it is worth bearing in mind that it may result in more work for you – and even occasional quarrels between you and the other occupiers of the block.

Extending your lease

An alternative for leaseholders who are worried about the falling value of their declining lease is to buy an extension to the lease. This is an easier process in many ways: you do not have to get two-thirds of your fellow-leaseholders to agree, and you may also qualify in circumstances which would rule you out of buying the freehold – for instance, if your flat is not in a self-contained block (a penthouse flat above offices would be one example). However, you must still be a 'qualifying tenant' under the terms of the Act, and must have lived there full-time, either for the last year, or any three years in the last 10.

Buying an extension to the lease will not allow you to escape high service charges or inefficient managing agents in the future, but it may add considerably to the value of your flat – or, indeed, simply make it saleable.

Once again, the Act lays down ground rules on how the lease extension should be valued. As a rule of thumb, the shorter your existing lease, the greater will be the price you must pay for an extension. As with purchasing the freehold, the buyer must pay the seller's legal costs.

Incidentally, although the Act rules certain people ineligible for the right to buy the freehold or extend the lease because of the nature of the property, this does not, of course, mean that such individuals *cannot* do so – only that they have no statutory right to do so. It may still be possible to negotiate such a sale.

Financing the cost

So long as you have some equity in your property, there should normally be no problem in adding the cost of the purchase to your existing mortgage, and paying it back over a normal mortgage term, at normal mortgage rates. If your current mortgage is for less than £30,000, the extra loan will qualify for MIRAS – mortgage interest relief – up to this limit. But it won't be so easy if your total mortgage takes you above 95% of the value of the property. In this case, an unsecured bank loan is likely to be the only option.

Buying a Houseboat

Many mainstream mortgage lenders will not touch houseboats – sorry! – with a barge-pole. Your bank may be able to help, but attitudes appear to differ widely; some of the high street banks just say 'no', others say 'maybe', depending on the particular circumstances. You may have to approach a specialized marine credit broker, although if you are buying the boat as a second home and have spare equity in your house, you may be able to arrange the loan with a conventional lender secured against your bricks and mortar.

For those who want to buy a houseboat as their main home, loans are available, but they are likely to be both more expensive and repayable over a shorter term than ordinary mortgages – a maximum loan of 80%, repayable over a term of 10 years or thereabouts, with interest rates currently around the 15% mark, compared with around 8.4% on an ordinary mortgage. One key point: you must have mooring rights organized before a loan will be made available.

'Self-Build': How to Finance It

Building your own home can work out 20 to 30% cheaper than buying an 'off the peg' new house, according to the experts and, of course, buyers get the house they really want. In addition, they save on VAT and on stamp duty (unless the plot of land itself costs in excess of £60,000).

A number of building societies, including Bradford & Bingley, Alliance & Leicester and Norwich & Peterborough, are all currently prepared to make mortgages available on self-build homes. Generally speaking, you will need to have enough cash to pay for the land outright and for 15 to 20% of the total building costs. The rest can be raised through ordinary mortgage, which is generally released in up to four stages, as the work progresses.

The monthly publication *Moneyfacts* gives details of all lenders currently in the market for self-build mortgages. Another useful source of information is the Self Build Advisory Centre, which runs regular seminars for those planning on building homes in the South-West of England. Elsewhere, the best initial source of information may be a manufacturer of 'package' kits, such as Potton. There is also a monthly magazine called *Individual Homes*, published by Centaur Publications. (For details, see Appendix, page 134.)

Buying a Second Home

The cottage in the country is a dream for many townies or suburbanites. What is the best way to finance it? The first option to consider is remortgaging your present property and raising the extra cash in this way. This has particular advantages if you are thinking of renting out the second home from time to time; most mortgage lenders are not very keen on this, and may even load the interest rate. So if you can keep the second home free of a mortgage charge, this is all to the good.

There are two further points to bear in mind if you plan to let the property on a regular basis. Assuming you do remortgage your main home, you should ask the lender to give you two separate accounts, one relating to the portion for your main home, one relating to the new property. This will allow you to identify for tax purposes the interest paid on your second home, as interest is usually allowed to be offset against rent received.

Secondly, do remember to tell your insurance company that the house is being let out. On both contents and buildings insurance, the insurer would be within its rights to turn down or underpay any claim if it had not been informed.

The second option for financing the purchase is to take out a mortgage directly on the second home. If you don't have sufficient equity in your first property, of course, this will be the only option. Some lenders are happy to lend on second homes; others are less keen, and may not allow borrowers buying second homes to take advantage of any special terms on offer. If this is the case, it is worth shopping around, and possibly consulting a mortgage broker, before you go ahead.

Buying Abroad

As with second homes in this country, buyers looking to finance the purchase of a property abroad have two options: either to take out a larger mortgage on their UK property, or to take out a loan secured on their overseas home.

If you choose the latter course, the next decision is whether to take out a loan in Sterling or in the local currency. If your income is wholly in Sterling, you should remember that currency fluctuations could make it difficult to plan ahead with a foreign currency loan.

The three largest lenders currently specializing in this area are Abbey National, Barclays and Woolwich. Deposits of 20% or more are generally required, and maximum loan terms tend to be rather shorter than in this country; 15 years is more likely than 25.

It is worth doing sums on both bases – extending the current mortgage on your British home, and taking out a separate loan on the foreign property – to see which will work out cheaper. If you are planning to let the overseas property, make sure the lender is aware of your plans.

There are numerous specialized books on buying properties in countries such as France, Spain and Portugal. The legal systems are very different in each country, so be prepared to do a certain amount of homework before you buy. You should also be prepared for extra costs: estate agents' fees and legal fees can be much more expensive in France than in the UK, for example.

Tax and Homes

If you are buying a second home you may well have to grapple with capital gains tax legislation. Under the current rules, any profit you make on the sale of your 'principal private residence' is free of capital gains tax. You do not have to have lived there all the time to qualify for this definition; if you have worked abroad for a number of years, for example, but have kept your home in this country, it still qualifies and no gains tax is payable. Another provision exempts people who have not lived there for the last three years of their ownership.

However, once you buy a country cottage or a second home, you must decide ('elect', to use the tax jargon) which of the two is your principal residence; selling the other could incur CGT. This election must be made within two years of buying the second property. In practice, many people with two homes will still escape the tax. If they buy a country cottage with a view to retiring there, they can eventually sell their main, town house free of CGT because it is their principal private residence at the time of the sale. The country cottage then becomes the principal residence and a subsequent sale would again be tax-free.

Suppose, however, you decided to sell up the country cottage before you had moved there full-time; in that case, a tax bill on any profit looks likely. If you think you might be in this position, it is worth scrupulously keeping all bills incurred both for the purchase and subsequent repairs or renovations. These expenses can be added to the original purchase price of the property; the higher this is, the lower the taxable profit you will have made. Remember, too, that one of the basic provisions of the CGT legislation is that inflation-only gains are stripped out before tax is paid. So you can scale up the purchase price, *and* the subsequent costs, by the amount of inflation which has prevailed since they were incurred, again cutting down on your taxable profit. Finally, don't forget that you may use the annual CGT exemption of £6,000 (£12,000 for a couple) to set against the profit.

It may be worth getting an accountant's help if, despite all these provisos, it looks as if you might be liable to some tax. But with relatively static property prices, most second-homeowners – especially if they have bought in the last few years – are unlikely to be hit by CGT. However, if you are contemplating buying abroad, remember that if you are resident in this country for tax purposes, any gains you make on the sale of your foreign property are also potentially liable for CGT.

One final point regarding tax and homes. If you work from home you should be careful how you phrase your claim for business expenses connected with the home. If you claim for expenses relating to a specific portion of the home – say, one complete room out of six – then, on sale, one sixth of the profit made will be taxable. However, if you have no specific area set aside, and simply claim a proportion of household expenses, then there should be no CGT liability.

10 | *Insurance and Your Home*

Once you've bought your home, there are three things that need to be insured: the house itself, your contents and, last but by no means least, you. The general message of this book has been to shop around for the best mortgage deals, but don't think you can relax now. It is almost as easy to waste money on insurance premiums as it is by choosing the wrong mortgage.

Insuring Your Life

The type of insurance policy you need to cover the mortgage depends on what sort of mortgage you choose. If you have opted for an endowment, no extra insurance is needed because it is all built into the policy. If you have a repayment loan, the cheapest option is a mortgage protection policy, which is also known as decreasing term assurance. Those with an interest-only or Pep mortgage would be best off with a level term assurance policy (see page 115).

Do you actually need this extra insurance? Many people belong to company pension schemes which provide life assurance cover of up to four times their salary if they die while they are working for their company. That sum should more than repay any existing mortgage, but remember that the cover stops immediately if you leave that company scheme. In any case, if you have dependants, you will probably need more insurance overall than the company scheme provides. All in all, it is a very sensible idea to take out insurance specifically to pay off the mortgage.

Mortgage protection policies

These last for the full term of the mortgage, but the sum assured – the amount that is paid out if you die within the term – declines each year to match the capital outstanding on the loan. Because the risk diminishes steadily over time, premiums are lower than for a 'level term' policy.

Most lenders, surprisingly enough, do not insist that you take out such a policy, but they are none the less keen to sell you one. Many of the big lenders these days have their own in-house insurance company; if not, a policy will be offered from the insurance company with which they have a 'tied' relationship.

Because the premium charged is relatively small compared to a mortgage payment, it may be tempting to take up the offer without thinking about it. But this is an area where independent advice can pay dividends. With any sort of term policy, remember, policy-holders get absolutely nothing back on their premiums if they survive for the full term, so by far the most important criterion on which to judge a policy is the size of the premiums.

Premiums vary according to your age and sex, the size of the initial sum assured, the term of the mortgage and, usually, whether or not you are a smoker. Occasionally insurance companies will charge different premiums for different occupations.

Do check whether the policy stipulates a maximum mortgage interest rate. With a repayment mortgage, as interest rates rise, the pace at which capital is paid back slows down. So if a policy says it will cover rates up to a maxium of 12% and mortgage rates rise to 15%, the amount still outstanding on the loan could be in excess of what the policy would pay out. Some companies have no limit on the interest rate; others vary between about 13 and 16%. It would be wise not to accept a policy which stipulates a maximum rate of less than 13%.

Table 28 gives two examples of the premiums that were current at the time of writing from a range of insurance companies. The first section of each example shows the best buys, and the second

Table 28: Cost of mortgage protection policies

Example (a)

Man aged 30, non-smoker, taking out a policy to cover a £60,000
repayment mortgage over 25 years

Company	Monthly premium	Mortgage rate*
Norwich Union	£7.80	16%
Zurich Life	£9.38	15%
Scottish Widows	£9.92	15%
Legal & General	£10.24	14%
Permanent	£10.44	**
Canada Life***	£10.58	13%
Halifax	£11.53	15%
Abbey National	£15.26	13%
Nationwide	£11.22	**

Example (b)

Couple aged 45 and 42, non-smokers, taking out a policy to cover a
£60,000 repayment mortgage over 20 years; policy to pay up in the
event of either death

Company	Monthly premium	Mortgage rate*
Canada Life***	£28.80	13%
Zurich Life	£29.41	15%
Scottish Widows	£30.38	15%
General Accident	£31.50	15%
Permanent	£32.39	**
Norwich Union	£34.20	16%
Halifax	£42.63	15%
Abbey National	£51.02	13%
Nationwide	£39.72	**

* *Maximum mortgage rate at which policy guarantees full cover of loan amount.*
** *Full cover guaranteed at any mortgage rate.*
*** *Premiums vary according to policyholder's occupation.*

Source: London & Country Mortgages

section shows the premiums charged on policies provided by three of the biggest mortgage lenders.

Of course, rates may change between the time of writing and your reading this, but the purpose of the table is really to alert you to the savings that can be made if you take the trouble to get independent advice. For instance, the man aged 30 borrowing £60,000 could be saving well over £1,200 during the term of the mortgage by choosing the cheapest policy rather than the most expensive; while for the couple in their 40s, savings could be in excess of £3,000.

Level term assurance

These policies pay out a fixed sum assured if you die within the term. This makes them the most suitable policy for people who take out a Pep mortgage, where the value of the Pep investment may fluctuate. Premiums are slightly more expensive than those for a mortgage protection policy at any given age; Table 29 gives some examples of current rates.

If you are self-employed you are allowed to use 5% of your net relevant earnings to pay premiums on a term assurance policy, and these premiums will qualify for full income tax relief. If you are in this situation it is worth getting independent advice as you will save between 25 and 40% on the premiums.

Accident, sickness and unemployment insurance

Insurance to cover mortgage payments if you are unable to work through accident or illness, or if you become unemployed, has become more important as the government has cut back its own help for borrowers in a bid to halt the growing expenditure – well over £1 billion a year – in this area.

Current government support depends on when the mortgage was taken out: if it was before 1 October 1995 one set of rules applies; if later, the rules change. For pre-October 1995 mortgages, those borrowers who become eligible for Income Support will not have their mortgage interest paid for the first two months, but thereafter 50% of the interest is paid for the following four months. At the end of that time the full mortgage interest is paid for as long as the claimant remains eligible for Income Support. The limits to the scheme are: firstly, interest is only paid on loans up to £100,000; and secondly, the payments do not cover any capital repayments or endowment premiums (or regular Pep savings).

Table 29: Cost of level term assurance policies

Example (a)
Man aged 30, non-smoker, taking out a policy for £60,000 for a term of 25 years

Company	Monthly premium
Prosperity	£10.06
Norwich Union	£10.80
Scottish Widows	£11.57
Commercial Union	£11.90
Permanent	£11.91
NPI	£16.72
Clerical Medical	£17.24
Scottish Life	£19.50

Example (b)
Couple aged 45 and 42, non-smokers, taking out a policy for £60,000 for a term of 25 years; policy to pay up in the event of either death

Company	Monthly premium
Scottish Widows	£39.02
Canada Life	£41.04
Zurich Life	£41.36
Permanent	£41.52
Royal	£41.56
NPI	£63.41
Clerical Medical	£66.08
Scottish Life	£81.66

Source: London & Country Mortgages

For mortgages taken out after that date, including remortgages, there will be no government help with mortgage interest at all for the first nine months after candidates become eligible for Income Support; thereafter 100% will be paid, subject to the overall £100,000 ceiling on loans.

There is no doubt that these cutbacks are a blow to many borrowers who are only just managing to finance their home-purchase, but it is worth pointing out that – according to government statistics at least – around 70% of borrowers who are off work through illness or unemployment are not eligible for Income Support in any case – either because their partner is still working, or because they have savings above a certain level. Savings of £8,000 or more mean you are disqualified completely from receiving help; with savings of more than £3,000 it will be limited.

Borrowers can fill the gap by taking out a specialist policy from their lender or mortgage broker when they take out their mortgage. Premiums will depend on the size of the monthly mortgage payment; with some policies borrowers are allowed to insure up to 125% of the monthly mortgage payment, so that endowment premiums, for example, can be covered as well.

Following the withdrawal of government help, these policies are rapidly being reviewed, but there are a number of areas which may prove problematical, and you should scour the small print – or ask the salesman – to find out the answers to the following questions:

- Is there a 'deferred period' before payments are made, for example the first three months of unemployment?
- How long will payments be made for – one year is currently typical for the unemployed, up to two years for those who cannot work through sickness or accident.
- Will it cover you for unemployment if you are on a short-term contract, work part-time or are self-employed?
- Are there are other restrictions? Some policies, for example, will not cover unemployment due to stress-related illnesses or alcohol abuse, or if you are sacked for misconduct.

In the past there have been numerous stories of people who have paid for such insurance and then, when the crunch came, found they were unable to claim due to some tortuous small print in the policy; it really is an area you should approach with care.

The cost of these policies is currently around £5 to £7 per month for each £100 of mortgage interest. However, these premiums may go down. At present the cost is influenced by the fact that it is voluntary, and buyers tend to be those who are most fearful of being made redundant. If everyone had such a policy, the risks – and the costs – might fall.

Insuring Your House

All mortgage lenders insist that your property is properly insured; nearly all of them will sell you an appropriate policy. You can insure with another company, but you are likely to be charged a one-off fee of £25 or thereabouts for doing so. Nevertheless, some shopping around through an insurance broker may provide substantial savings.

Premiums are based on the rebuilding cost for your property. It excludes the cost of the land, but owners of old houses – and especially of listed property – may well find the rebuilding cost is in excess of the purchase price.

The Building Cost Information Service, part of the Royal Institution of Chartered Surveyors (RICS; see Appendix, page 132) provides a rebuilding index used by most lenders; this divides properties into various types – detached, semis, terraced and so on – their ages, and their location. Thus, according to the latest figures, a 1980s-built large detached house in London would cost £54 per square foot to rebuild, while a small mid-Victorian terrace in the North-West would cost £61.50 per square foot. The Association of British Insurers (see Appendix, page 133) provides a free information leaflet entitled *How to Work Out the Rebuilding Cost of Your Home* (send a stamped addressed envelope).

While the insurance premiums are based on the rebuilding cost, the rate will depend on the location of the property and, in particular, the type of soil on which it is built. Houses built on clay, near cliffs or rivers which make a habit of bursting their banks, will attract higher premiums than property built out of the way of water on granite.

Insurance companies are beginning to use geological maps to price their risks more accurately, but some are still lagging behind. If you suspect your home is being rated too highly because of its proximity to land which qualifies as higher risk (because of flood danger, for example), try another insurance company; if this one uses more accurate maps you may get a substantially lower premium.

Small print to watch out for in buildings insurance includes whether the policy covers the cost of alternative accommodation if the home is destroyed; whether, and to what extent, it provides cover for fences, driveways, garden sheds, etc. Also check to see what, if any, 'excess' (the amount policholders must meet out of their own pockets) is imposed where the house suffers subsidence. It can be £500 or £1,000 or more.

If you have a home that is in any way unusual – a thatched cottage or a period, listed property – you may need specialized insurance. A good insurance broker may be helpful in this respect. The British Insurance and Investment Brokers Association (see Appendix, page 133) can provide names and addresses of qualified brokers.

One final point to remember: if you add to or improve the property in any way you must let the insurance company know. If the property is under-insured, insurers have the right to cut down on any claim by the same proportion, a process known as 'averaging'.

Buildings insurance for flats

This is normally organized by the freeholder or the managing agents. The mortgage lender, however, usually wants to see the policy to check it is adequate. Leaseholders pay their individual share of the premium to the freeholder – generally once a year.

Contents Insurance

It is up to you whether to arrange contents insurance; mortgage lenders do not insist on it. What determines the premium rate for contents insurance, more than anything else, is the likelihood of your house being burgled. Premiums vary wildly from about £3 per £1,000 sum insured in areas which are low risk for theft, up to £15 or even £20 per £1,000 for high risk (generally inner-city) areas.

By the same token, many insurance companies will offer discounts for security measures such as a burglar alarm, approved window and door locks, membership of a neighbourhood watch scheme, even ownership of a dog – and they do not specify that it has to be a fierce one!

One point not always appreciated by policyholders is that insurance companies base their premiums largely on their own experience of claims. So if your premium rises sharply from one year to the next, and you have not made any claim, it may well be because your insurers have had a number of claims from other policyholders in your area. It is worth ringing around a few other companies to see if you can get a better deal.

Another point to remember is that these insurance policies are, generally, set for one year only. At the end of that time, the company is free to change not just premium rates but also the terms of the policy, increasing the excess, for example, or withdrawing certain items from cover. That means you really should read the stuff that comes with the renewal form each year.

The sum assured under most policies is automatically index-linked, but if you have bought a significant number of extra items during the year the onus is on you to increase the sum assured accordingly. Otherwise the company may invoke its right to average down any claim.

As with other types of insurance policy, there will be restrictions and exclusions. Check to see what limit is put on the amount that can be claimed for especially valuable items – unless specified, they are generally restricted to 5% of the total sum insured. For your own protection it is worth taking photographs of such items, keeping receipts and a note of any serial number, and possibly getting items such as bicycles 'post-coded'.

Cover for accidental damage is usually optional and involves an extra premium, as does an 'all risks' extension, providing cover on items taken out of the home. These days insurers are keen to organize repairs of damaged items rather than provide the money for replacements – they are within their rights to do so.

Finally, most policies are now on a 'new for old' basis, which provides sufficient cover for replacing damaged, destroyed or burgled items with new ones. The alternative is an 'indemnity' basis, which only pays the second-hand value of goods lost. However, whichever basis is used, clothes and household linen are generally priced at their second-hand value.

In the event of a large claim, the insurance company may send in a loss adjustor to assess the loss on its behalf. You, in turn, can employ a loss assessor to fight your corner of the case – or if you use a firm of insurance brokers, they may fulfil this function for you.

Shopping around

These days anyone seriously interested in getting the best value insurance deal must go to a number of sources: mortgage lenders, as mentioned above, who offer their own policies; independent insurance brokers or other advisers, who will be able to search the conventional insurance market on your behalf; and a growing number of direct insurers dealing solely by telephone.

Insurance problems

Most insurance companies belong to the Insurance Ombudsman Bureau (see Appendix, page 135), an independent body whose function is to adjudicate in quarrels between insurers and their policyholders. The service is free to policyholders and does not prejudice their rights to take the company to the courts.

11 ‖ *In the Future: Moving and Improving*

Moving

One of the basic pieces of advice offered in this book is that you should choose your first property to 'last' you for more than two or three years. The expenses incurred in buying and selling, the uncertainty of finding a buyer, the likelihood these days that your own property will not have risen markedly in value over just a couple of years – all these factors make it wise to choose well first time round.

Nevertheless, there will almost inevitably come a point in your life where you either want or need to move. Many large companies still need managers who trek around the country doing jobs in different branch offices for a number of years. With luck, your company will offer a decent relocation package; and so it should. Ideally, it should finance both the cost of the sale and purchase (plus removals and so on) and also any time-lag between buying your new home and selling the old one.

Planning your move

These days you should try to line up a buyer for your old home before committing yourself to the purchase of a new one. Easier said than done, of course, but not only will it save you the agony of uncertainty, and potentially expensive bridging loans; it will put you in an excellent bargaining position as a cash buyer. Even if it means spending a few months in rented accommodation, it may still be the best decision. Desperate sellers can resort to auctions, but 'forced sale' prices are, almost by definition, much lower than prices obtained in normal situations.

Using an estate agent

Sellers can advertise property themselves, but the usual course of action is to place it with an estate agent. Expect to pay between 1 and 2.5% of the sale price for a 'sole agency' agreement, where you promise not to put the property with a second company, and between 2 and 3.5% if you are using two or more firms.

It would seem sensible, at least initially, to place the property on a sole agency basis. Ask around to find out which is the most active and efficient agent in your area, or simply carry out your own survey of 'For Sale' and 'Sold' boards.

You will need to establish exactly what the agent's fees will cover, whether it includes advertising (if so, how much?), and what sort of details of the property will be produced. Unusual and expensive properties may have a whole brochure devoted to them; in this case, the price will depend on individual negotiations between agent and client. It is in any case a good idea to get the agreement between yourselves and the agent in writing.

Showing people round

Most sellers prefer to show round potential buyers themselves, even if they are using an estate agent. You will find you quickly develop a routine, but a little bit of preparation is required.

Firstly, have facts and figures at your fingertips. These should include:

- the band in which the house falls for council tax purposes, and the amount payable
- the size of the water bills
- the ground rent and latest service charges for a flat
- heating bills over the last two years or so
- details of any structural work undertaken recently, and any guarantees on it you might have
- details of matters not immediately obvious to a buyer – for example, the quality of loft insulation, or the last time the chimneys were swept.

Bearing in mind that some potential buyers may be coming from outside the immediate area, be prepared to be a sort of travel rep for your locality, with accurate information on the proximity of schools, shops, hospitals and public transport.

Secondly, give your house and garden the best possible beauty treatment before you start. Well-placed furniture adds to the perceived space available, while clutter deducts from it. Remember that builders of new houses don't equip a show-house purely for the fun of it, but because it genuinely helps sales.

So banish your clutter as far as possible – making a mental note not to put it in some wardrobe that you are later going to fling open to demonstrate the size of storage space, only to be engulfed in a deluge of dirty laundry. The bathroom is particularly important: in modern houses it is often rather a poky room; in Victorian ones it may have been squeezed out of half a spare bedroom. So be brave and throw out that clutter of bottles, moth-eaten sponges and loofahs. The room will look the better for it.

Next to tidiness – or even before it – is cleanliness. Nearly everyone looks forward to putting up their own pictures and ornaments, even redecorating, to make a place their own. No one – at least in my experience – looks forward to cleaning up dirt, and especially not someone else's. A bit of dust is nothing, but dirty windows are seriously bad news. And as for smells . . .

Some people think that using something akin to the old super- market trick of spraying a 'fresh bread' smell near the loaves is a bit too obvious. Certainly a house that smells strongly of some ghastly air freshener is likely to cause positive alarm in potential buyers – they will be convinced that there must be something wrong with the drains.

But it should not be beyond the bounds of your ingenuity to get the place smelling reasonably pleasant. If you make your viewers coffee, for instance, make sure it's real coffee. And be hard- hearted where cats and dogs are concerned: banish them if poss- ible. Gardens should be kept trim, especially front gardens, where the all-important first impression is created. If you are selling in winter, have a few photographs available to show what the garden looks like in the spring and summer.

Be as friendly and helpful as you can, but don't talk too much. By all means take the visitors on a 'guided tour', but then let them have some space to themselves. They may well want to go round on their own a second time, so make sure that any obvious valuables – jewellery and so on – are safely locked away.

And finally, whatever you might really feel about the place, never, *ever* apologize.

Selling by auction

If you are desperate to sell, and sell quickly, you can consider putting your property up for auction. With reasonable luck you should be guaranteed a fast sale – but, of course, a lower price. Auctioneers say that sellers should expect to get around 20% less by selling through auction; on the other hand, 80% of properties put up for sale sell either before or on the day of the auction.

Do some homework before choosing your auctioneer, and be prepared for some substantial costs – it may prove to be no cheaper than selling through an estate agent.

The Incorporated Society of Valuers and Auctioneers (ISVA; see Appendix, page 132) will provide a list of its members who organize property auctions. Before choosing a firm, ask what its average 'success rate' is. Be prepared to take the auctioneer's advice on a realistic 'reserve price' (the lowest amount you are prepared to sell for) as well as the 'guide price' (the amount that will be quoted in the catalogue).

Auctions still deal largely with the 'difficult to sell' properties: those which have problems of one sort or another – they may just be badly run-down, or in a difficult location, or have a sitting tenant. Probate property, or homes which have been repossessed by a mortgage lender, are often sold at auction. But with the property market so quiet at the moment, 'ordinary' sellers are increasingly favouring this option as well.

Staying Where You Are and Improving

Many people decide that moving is just too much hassle – and one can hardly blame them. Instead, they may opt to 'save' money by escaping all those buying and selling expenses and devote the cash to improving their present property.

Home improvements fall into three distinct categories: those that add value to your home; those which are neutral; and those which can actually make it less valuable, or at least make it more difficult to sell.

You don't have to become an aficionado of style to decide on the right improvements, but be warned, style *does* matter. Nasty modern windows on an unpretentious Edwardian terrace, a vast Regency-style pillared porch tacked onto a 1960s 'box', or (that most notorious of 'improvements') stone cladding, can all be a hindrance when you come to sell your place later, and may mean a lower price.

Given the wide range of styles and ages of properties, it is impossible to come up with any general rules, except to say that you should, if possible, aim for harmony. Whatever you do should 'fit in' with what is there already – though this does not necessarily mean that only slavish imitation is allowed. If you live in a listed house or a conservation area, this approach will be forced on you in any case, as you must follow the planning rules or risk all sorts of trouble and expense, including being forced to re-do all your improvements properly or undo them altogether.

The Woolwich Building Society has graded the main improvements anyone is likely to make on the basis of their potential for adding value. The best are as follows, with marks out of 10 being awarded:

- **Refitting the kitchen** – going from worst to best, this counts as 8 out of 10, and is worth spending money on.
- **Adding a garage** – 7 out of 10. For many houses – for example terraces – adding a garage is out of the question. If you can, however, it will undoubtedly add to a property's saleability.

- **Adding a conservatory** – 6 out of 10. The main pitfall here is opting for a style that is grossly out of keeping with the existing property.
- **Insulation** – 6 out of 10. Half of British homes do not have thick enough insulation in the loft, while only one in five of those with cavity walls have had them insulated. Putting both these matters right will recoup homeowners' costs within a few years by reducing heating bills.
- **Building an extension** – 6 out of 10. The cardinal rule, as with a conservatory, is to aim for a style in keeping with your house. Remember, however beautiful the extension, the main factor governing any house price is its position. 'Over-improving' for your area may be a financial trap.
- **Bathroom renewal** – 6 out of 10, but beware of choosing a colour that may not go down well with potential buyers. White is safest.
- **Replacing window frames** – 5 out of 10. There is a trend towards 'maintenance-free' frames but once again the style is all important. Nothing detracts so immediately from the appearance of a house as the 'wrong' windows.

Also meriting 5 out of 10 are, perhaps surprisingly, redecoration and restoration of period features, while loft conversions are only awarded 4 out of 10.

The best home improvement, however, is installing central heating which gets a 10 out of 10. If you are installing or replacing a central heating system, it may be worth spending extra money to buy an energy-efficient gas condensing boiler which could save between 20 and 40% on current fuel bills.

Clearly, these are generalizations. Most people undertake home improvements to suit themselves rather than potential buyers, but even if you expect to live somewhere a good long time, it is worth considering what others might think of your pet project before going ahead.

Planning permission

Neglect this at your peril. The Department of the Environment publishes a number of useful booklets detailing the circumstances where permission is required; there is one which deals specifically with satellite dishes. *Planning – A Guide for Householders* gives general guidance on when planning permission must be sought, but homeowners should check with their local council as well. The council will usually give informal advice, but if you want a formal ruling on the matter you can apply to the council for a 'determination' by writing to them with details of the intended work.

The following guidelines apply where the house is neither listed nor in a conservation area. In such cases most minor (and many not so minor) alterations or additions do not usually need planning permission, but it is always sensible to check because the rules can be quite complicated and other factors may be involved which make planning permission necessary:

- **Extensions**: planning permission required only if the proposed extension adds more than 10% to the original volume of a terraced house, or 15% to a semi or a detached house.
- **Roof lights and skylights**: planning permission not necessary.
- **Loft conversions or extensions**: planning permission required if it adds more than 50 cubic metres to the volume of the house, 40 in the case of a terraced house. Special rules apply to the insertion of dormer windows.
- **Adding a porch**: not usually required, but once again there are detailed rules here and if, for example, the porch would be less than two metres away from a road, planning permission will be required.
- **Internal decorations, alterations or insertion of windows**: planning permission not required – but special rules apply to bay windows.

However, planning permission is always required if your plans involve making part of your house a self-contained residential unit, or a self-contained workshop or office for business or commercial use.

Rules for those living in a conservation area can be more stringent, while those for listed buildings are very strict: in these cases it is essential to check with the council first.

Remember that other kinds of permission may be required – for example if the work involves pruning or felling trees that are protected by a preservation order.

Building regulations approval

This is another type of 'permission' quite separate from planning permission. These regulations exist mainly to prevent botched jobs or D I Y disasters, but you can end up in court and pay fines of up to £2,000 if work is carried out illegally without appropriate permission.

Building regulations approval is required if you intend to:

- convert your home into flats
- convert the loft
- carry out some major repairs such as removing most of a wall to rebuild it
- build a large extension (but not, for example, a small porch or conservatory).

You do not need building regulations approval for minor repairs such as rewiring, replacing windows or replacing the felt to a flat roof.

How to pay for home improvements

In terms of the interest rate, the cheapest way to finance home improvements is to increase your mortgage. Most lenders will charge the same rate on the additional sum as they do on the original mortgage, though some may impose a loading of perhaps 1%. If you are thinking of taking out a significant additional loan it may be a good idea to consider remortgaging the whole lot in any case – you may be able to pick up a better overall deal from a new lender.

There are three possible drawbacks to this route. One: you have to have sufficient equity in your property to back the additional loan, otherwise you will not get a mortgage at all. Two: if your equity is less than 25% of the property value you will have the extra cost of paying for a mortgage indemnity guarantee (see page 81). And three: you will in any case have to pay for a fresh valuation of the property, which may set you back a few hundred pounds – Table 2 (see page 29) gives an indication of when this is likely to be.

One last thing to think about if you are considering adding to your existing mortgage rather than remortgaging overall: normally, lenders will expect the additional loan to be repaid at the same time as the rest of the mortgage. This may suit you, but you may find it either too long or too short a term and therefore prefer to go for a personal loan instead which, because it is not secured on your property, does not require equity or a fee for a new valuation. By the same token, however, interest rates will be higher. At the time of writing, while the basic mortgage rate is around 8.4%, rates for unsecured personal loans stand at 15 to 18%. The term generally ranges from one to five years, and the amount that can be borrowed (depending on the lender) from £500 or £1,000 to a maximum of £15,000.

A third option, offered by many mortgage lenders, is a secured personal loan. Interest rates for this option are currently around 13 or 14%. Secured personal loans usually require a revaluation of the property, but the fee may be lower than the lender's normal fee for valuations on purchase.

When choosing, it is also worth checking out what your bank has to offer.

Insurance

Finally, if you are contemplating extensive works, don't forget to get them insured from the start, rather than when the works are completed; if your three-quarters built extension were to be destroyed you could face significant loss.

THE LAST WORD

Buying a home is the biggest purchase most of us will ever make. It is very expensive, it takes a long time to repay, and we have to live in it in the meantime. All obvious points, of course – but I am continually surprised by the attitude of some people, who behave as if the purchase (or at least, its financial aspects) deserved little more consideration than buying a car.

Many people may be unwilling to ask too many questions because they suspect they will not understand the answers; but the only remedy to that, which I would urge on everyone, is simply to keep on asking until you get an intelligible reply.

The choices confronting the homebuyer today do not necessarily have a 'right' answer – only a number of possible courses of action where only you can decide, finally, what is appropriate for you. Nevertheless, it is useful to try and summarize the main aspects of house-buying, and boil them all down into five neat 'golden rules'.

The Five Golden Rules of House Purchase

1. Buy somewhere you really want to live in – not just now, but in five or 10-years' time.
2. Save up for a decent-sized deposit – 10% – before you buy.
3. Repay capital as you go; either by means of a formal repayment mortgage or by putting in occasional lump sums.
4. Spend sufficient money to maintain the property in a sound structural condition.
5. Shop around for your mortgage and your insurance. It could save you a small fortune.

APPENDIX

Useful Addresses and Contact Numbers

General
Building Societies Association/Council of Mortgage Lenders
3 Savile Row
London W1X 1AF
0171 437 0655

Publishes a number of free booklets on mortgages and moving home.

Estate agents, valuations, surveys

National Association of Estate Agents
Arbon House
21 Jury Street
Warwick CV34 4EH
01926 496800

Royal Institution of Chartered Surveyors (RICS)
12 Great George Street
London SW1P 3AE
0171 222 700

Incorporated Society of Valuers & Auctioneers (ISVA)
3 Cadogan Gate
London SW1X 0AS
0171 235 2282

Association of Relocation Agents
Premier House
11 Marlborough Place
Brighton BN1 1UB
01273 624455

Insurance matters

Association of British Insurers
51 Gresham Street
London EC2V 7HQ
0171 600 3333

Publishes a number of free information leaflets on insuring your home and contents.

British Insurance and Investment Brokers Association
  (BIIBA)
14 Bevis Marks
London EC3A 7NT
0171 623 9043

Provides names and addresses of insurance brokers.

Where to sell endowment policies

Association of Policy Marketmakers
Holywell Centre
1 Phipp Street
London EC2A 4PS
0171 739 3949

Provides free information brochure plus list of members.

Credit information agencies

CCN Group
Consumer Help Service
PO Box 40
Nottingham NG7 2SS

Equifax Europe (UK) Ltd
Consumer Affairs Department
Spectrum House
1a North Avenue
Clydebank
Glasgow G81 2DR

Information on self-building

Self Build Advisory Centre
8 New North Road
Exeter EX4 4HH
01392 499727

Potton Group
Willow Road
Potton
Sandy
Bedfordshire SG19 2PP
01767 260348

Publications

Moneyfacts magazine
Laundry Loke
North Walsham
Norfolk NR28 0BD
01692 500765

Individual Homes magazine
Centaur Publications
Assent Publishing
91–93 High Street
Bromsgrove
Worcestershire B61 8AQ
01527 836600

Where to complain

Just about every area of financial services has its own
ombudsman or formal complaints system, but it should be noted
that some types of complaint may be outside their jurisdiction.
The main ones are as follows:

Building Society Ombudsman
Grosvenor Gardens House
35–37 Grosvenor Gardens
London SW1X 7AW
0171 931 0044

Deals with complaints against all building societies but does not include, for example, the decision whether or not to give someone a mortgage.

Banking Ombudsman
70 Gray's Inn Road
London WC1X 8NB
0171 404 9944

Covers all major high street banks.

Ombudsman for Corporate Estate Agents
Beckett House
4 Bridge Street
Salisbury
Wiltshire SP1 2LX

Deals with complaints arising from dealings with some large chains of estate agents.

Insurance Ombudsman Bureau
City Gate One
135 Park Street
London SE1 9EA
0171 928 7600

Deals with complaints about non-life insurance, including buildings and contents, motor and medical insurance.

Personal Investment Authority Ombudsman
3rd Floor
Centrepoint
103 New Oxford Street
London WC1A 1QH
0171 379 0444

Deals with complaints about financial advisers, life and pensions products and sometimes unit trusts and Peps.

Investment Ombudsman
6 Frederick's Place
London EC2R 8BT
0171 796 3065

Covers most complaints relating to investment trusts, unit trusts and Peps. There may be overlap with the PIA ombudsman; the nature of the complaint will decide whether it will be heard by the Investment Ombudsman or the PIA one.

Pensions Ombudsman
11 Belgrave Road
London SW1V 1RB
0171 233 8080

Covers many complaints relating to company or personal pensions; some – such as complaints of mis-selling – may be dealt with by the PIA ombudsman.

Solicitors' Complaints Bureau
Victoria Court
8 Dormer Place
Leamington Spa
Warwickshire CV32 5AE
01926 820082

Deals with matters relating to solicitors' conduct. A Legal Services Ombudsman may be appealed to if complainants are dissatisfied with the result.

INDEX

The Sunday Times Personal Finance Guide to Tax-free Savings

How to Make Your Money Work Hardest For You

Christopher Gilchrist

Are you making the most of your savings and investments?

Nobody enjoys paying tax but few people make full use of the many opportunities now available to everyone in the UK to save and invest tax-free. This guide explains the basics of tax and investment and shows how you can use tax-free plans to make more of your money, including:

- how moving your savings into tax-free schemes can boost your returns
- how to work out what you need to save for retirement and the best tax-exempt ways to do so
- the differences between lower-risk, moderate-risk and high-risk schemes and how much each could produce for you
- identifying the saving and investment plans that offer the best value for money
- the best plans for short-term and longer-term savings

Over a period of twenty years, £100 a month placed in a building society account might accumulate to £45,000. But a good tax-exempt savings plan linked to shares could turn that same £100 a month into £130,000.

Taking the right decisions now on where to save your surplus income could add tens of thousands of pounds to your personal wealth.

0 00 638703 9

HarperCollinsPaperbacks

The Sunday Times
Personal Finance Guide to
The Protection Game
A Straightforward Guide to Insurance

Kevin Pratt

Do you have adequate insurance protection and are you getting good value for your premiums?

The Protection Game covers the whole gamut of insurance products, from simple life cover, medical plans and income replacement schemes through to motor and household protection contracts. It is designed to help you build a portfolio of policies that will protect you and your family from the mishaps, misfortunes and tragedies that life so often has to offer.

This guide examines the various insurance policies on the market, describing how they are sold and what they are intended to cover. It cuts through the jargon that often surrounds this area and outlines why and how particular products are appropriate to particular circumstances. *The Protection Game* enables you to:

- remove the mystery and cut through the complexity of insurance
- discover where to get the best value for money
- protect your belongings, your home and your family
- find out what to do when things go wrong

In short, *The Protection Game* addresses everything you need to obtain the priceless gift of peace of mind.

0 00 638702 0

HarperCollinsPaperbacks

The Sunday Times Personal Finance Guide to Your Pension

How to Invest for Future Security

Stephen Ellis

Are you aware of the various pension schemes available?
Do you know how best to ensure a secure financial future when you retire?

Twenty years ago most people did not give their pensions a second thought. But today people of all ages are aware that their pension is likely to be the biggest investment they will ever make. The realization that the State is not going to support everyone in old age has forced people to acknowledge that pensions are crucially important. Moreover, increasingly flexible work patterns mean that the onus is on the individual as much as on the employer to initiate plans for future security.

This guide shows how to plan for your income and investments in retirement and tackles the following issues:

- What will State pensions provide?
- How do company pension schemes work and what will they pay?
- Once retired what measures can you take to ensure maximum use of your income?

Your Pension – How to Invest for Future Security is a concise and accessible guide which illuminates the way to retirement with a minimum of financial worries.

0 00 638705 5

HarperCollinsPaperbacks

The Sunday Times Personal Finance Guide to Your Retirement

How to Plan Wisely for Later Life

Diana Wright

Are you approaching retirement? Do you know:

- How much your pension will be?
- How to trace pensions from previous employers?
- Whether you should take the lump sum from your pension scheme?
- What sort of annuity you should buy and what difference a good choice would make?
- How to rebalance your investment portfolio to suit life after work?
- Where to find good financial advice?
- What sort of insurance you need?

Your Retirement – How to Plan Wisely for Later Life is a practical, informative guide for anyone nearing the end of their working lives. You do not have to be an expert in financial matters to take advantage of the opportunities available. This guide covers an entire range of options including tax planning – how to make the best use of tax-exempt investments, how to avoid the 'age allowance trap' and how to plan for inheritance tax; how to use your home to provide an income; and how some people can improve their pension income by ten per cent or more by making one simple move.

0 00 638707 1

HarperCollinsPaperbacks